# Just Add Puppets

# 20 Instant
# Puppet Skits
## for Children's Ministry

# Group
Loveland, Colorado

## Group's R.E.A.L. Guarantee to you:

Every Group resource incorporates our R.E.A.L. approach to ministry—a unique philosophy that results in long-term retention and life transformation. It's ministry that's:

**This is EARL. He's R.E.A.L. mixed up. (Get it?)**

**Relational**
Because student-to-student interaction enhances learning and builds Christian friendships.

**Experiential**
Because what students experience sticks with them up to 9 times longer than what they simply hear or read.

**Applicable**
Because the aim of Christian education is to be both hearers and doers of the Word.

**Learner-based**
Because students learn more and retain it longer when the process is designed according to how they learn best.

**Just Add Puppets: 20 Instant Puppet Skits for Children's Ministry**

Copyright © 2001 Group Publishing, Inc.

Visit our Web site: **www.grouppublishing.com**

**Credits**
Authors: Steve and Cora Alley, Peggy Bradshaw, and Debbie Freeman
Editors: Linda Anderson and Cindy S. Hansen
Creative Development Editors: Jan Kershner and Karl Leuthauser
Chief Creative Officer: Joani Schultz
Copy Editor: Lyndsay E. Bierce
Art Directors: Julia Ryan and Jean Bruns
Designer: Julia Ryan
Computer Graphic Artist: Tracy K. Donaldson
Illustrator: Megan Jeffery
Cover Art Director: Jeff A. Storm
Cover Designer: Lisa Chandler
Production Manager: Peggy Naylor
Puppet provided by One Way Street, Inc., www.onewaystreet.com, 800-569-4537

**Library of Congress Cataloging-in-Publication Data**
Just add puppets : 20 instant puppet skits for children's ministry.
    p.  cm.
   Includes indexes.
   ISBN 0-7644-2305-3 (alk. paper)
    1. Puppet theater in Christian education. I. Group Publishing.

BV1535.9.P8 J87 2001
246'.725--dc21

                                        2001033035
10 9 8 7 6 5 4 3      10 09 08 07 06 05 04 03
Printed in the United States of America.

# Contents

# Introduction

Children of all ages love puppets—whether kids are watching a puppet show or actually being the puppeteers. Puppets have a way of imparting biblical truths in a fun, humorous, and unforgettable way.

*Just Add Puppets* gives you twenty new skits that not only use puppets but also involve children in the audience. Most of the preparation is already done, since all the spoken dialogue, sound effects, and music are prerecorded and included on the CDs. The book includes suggested actions, costumes, props, and scenery, as well as a Scripture index and a topical index. It's never been so easy to put on a puppet show!

Audiences can enjoy *Just Add Puppets* in a variety of settings:

- a Sunday school class,
- a children's church gathering,
- a worship service,
- a family evening program,
- a community outreach event, or
- a special children's event.

*Just Add Puppets* can also be used in conjunction with Group Publishing's FaithWeaver™ Bible Curriculum and KidsOwn Worship™ for Summer 2001 through Summer 2002, which you can order from Group Publishing or your local Christian bookstore. Using *Just Add Puppets* along with this family ministry curriculum helps you reinforce Bible stories, verses, and themes in a way that cements Bible truths in kids' lives.

**Read on for some more fun tips about how to use *Just Add Puppets*.**

## Children's Church Connection

The puppet skits in *Just Add Puppets* connect well with any Sunday school program. However, special care has been taken to ensure that each skit connects with a lesson from Group Publishing's KidsOwn Worship™. There are four skits for each quarter from Summer 2001 to Summer 2002 that will help drive home the point you teach in KidsOwn Worship™ lessons. If you'd like to learn more about KidsOwn Worship™, check out www.faithweaver.com.

## Simple Steps to Perform a Skit

**1.** Gather kids who are interested in organizing a puppet skit.

**2.** Decide when and where to perform the skit.

**3.** Skim the topical index (p. 141) or the Scripture index (p. 141), and decide which skit will fit the purpose of your gathering.

**4.** Listen to the CD, then assign roles. You'll need kids to manipulate the puppets as well as make scene and prop changes.

**5.** Have kids help you collect and create costumes, props, and scenes. Many items can be collected from your church or from kids' homes.

**6.** Practice the skit with the kids, and synchronize the puppet movements with the CD. Some skits require stopping the CD while a leader asks the audience questions. Be familiar with the stops and starts of the CD.

**7.** Then on with the show! It's that simple.

**Here are a few additional tips to help you achieve an outstanding puppet performance!**

## Supplies Listing

Each skit includes a list of simple and easy-to-collect props. (Since all skits involve a stage, puppets, CD, and CD player, these aren't included in the list.) Involve kids every step of the way! Teenagers and senior adults might want to assist children in the puppet skit production. Volunteers can help as supply-gatherers, prop-handlers, costumers, actors, or directors.

## The Puppet Stage

You may already have an elaborate puppet stage, complete with background and foreground curtains. If so, rejoice! If not, rejoice anyway! There are easy ways to make a stage. Here's how:

- have puppeteers hold up a blanket and puppets perform behind it;
- turn a table on its side, and let the action begin;
- cut a stage out of a refrigerator box;
- ask a carpenter to build a stage out of wood; or
- build a stage out of plastic pipe and black curtains.

We've also included three background templates on pages 7-9. Photocopy each background on an overhead transparency, then use an overhead projector to project the image onto your background area. Trace and color the outline. The three basic backgrounds can be used in a variety of the skits in this book. Remember that your puppet stage can be as simple or elaborate as you want. You can do it!

## Staging Terms

Some staging terms are used in the scripts. "Downstage" is toward the front of the puppet stage, the area closest to the audience. "Upstage" is toward the back of the stage. "Stage left" is the left side of the stage as puppeteers face the audience. "Stage right" is the right side of the stage as puppeteers face the audience. "Center stage" is the middle section of the stage.

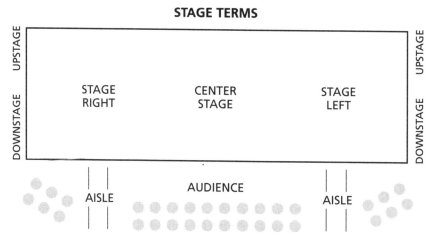

## The Puppets and Props

All of the skit directions are written assuming you have puppets with hands. If so, you can attach props by using Velcro, rubber bands, tape, or pins. However, these skits work with *any kind* of puppets, whether they're made with felt, paper sacks, or paper plates. If the puppets you're using have no hands, simply tape or pin the props to the front of each puppet. Or you could have puppeteers hold the props so that it looks as if the puppets are holding them, but the puppeteers' hands need to be out of view from the audience.

## Openings, Closings, and Scene Changes

The CDs include music or sound effects before and after each skit. The CDs also include a thirty-second music interlude for scene changes. If you need more time for a scene change, pause the CD.

If you have one, a spotlight works well for openings, closings, scene changes, and discussions. Turn it on for an opening, off for a scene change, on for the next scene, off for a discussion, and so forth. You don't have to use an expensive spotlight—a flashlight or a garage light works just as easily. Or, if you have curtains on a puppet stage, opening and closing the curtains works well for scene changes too.

**So...Lights! Camera! Action! Open *Just Add Puppets*, and on with the show.**

# Playground

# Living Room

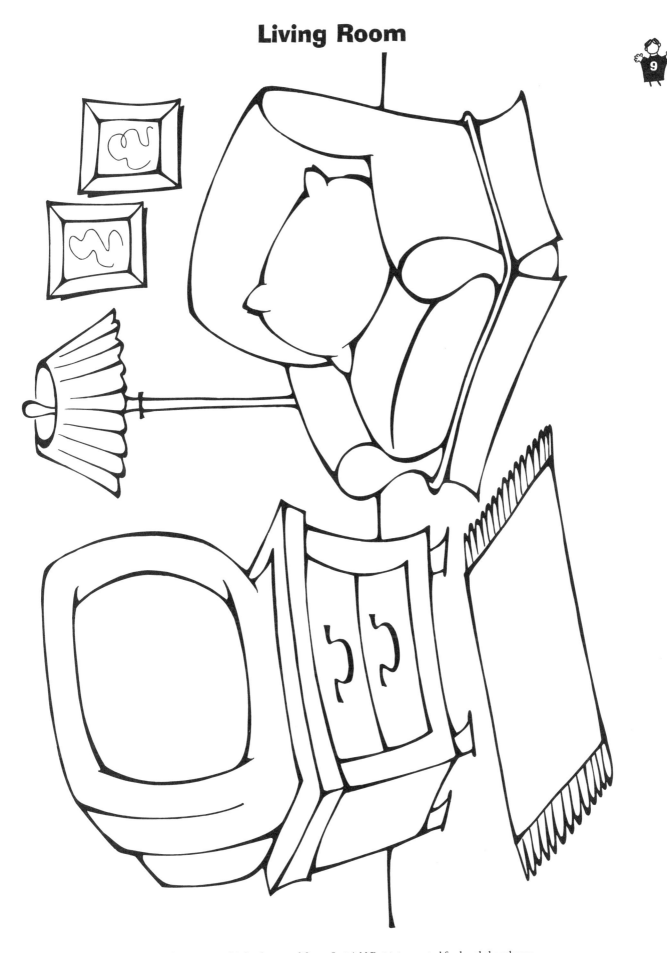

**Props for
"God Rules!"
(p. 53)**

**Props for
"God Rules!"
(p. 53)**

**Prop for
"God Rules!"
(p. 53)**

**Prop for
"Smelly Belly"
(p. 123)**

**Props for "Smelly Belly"**
**(p. 123)**

# Heartbeat

**Topic:** Prayer
**Scriptures You Might Read:** 1 Samuel 1; Matthew 6:5-13

**Scene 1:** Zachary's bedroom with a picture frame and Zachary's bed
**Scene 2:** The school playground

> **Teacher Tip** Cut a large heart out of construction paper, and attach it to a stick. Have someone hold it behind the puppet stage. Have the person raise the heart and wiggle it to the beat of each heartbeat sound on the CD.

## Characters
**ZACHARY:** a boy who is learning the true meaning of prayer
**BETTY:** a girl who helps Zachary learn a lesson
**MOM'S VOICE:** heard offstage

**Props:** You'll need one sheet of paper, one paper bag, one unwrapped granola bar, the bedroom background (p. 7), and the playground background (p. 8).

**Setup:** Attach a sheet of paper to Zachary's hand for the first scene. Be ready to attach an unwrapped granola bar to his hand for the second scene. Attach a lunch sack to Betty's hand, and have her ready for the second scene.

Before the skit, have the audience practice making a heartbeat sound. Have each person place one hand about six inches from his or her chest and slap the other hand between the hand and chest. Tell the audience to make the sound every time they hear the heartbeat on the CD.

## SCRIPT

| ACTIONS | WORDS |
| --- | --- |

 *Play track 1 on CD A.*

### SCENE 1: Zachary's Room

 *Play track 2 on CD A.*

| ACTIONS | WORDS |
| --- | --- |
| ZACHARY is in his bedroom, sitting on his bed, looking at the sheet of paper attached to his hand (notes for his science test). | **ZACHARY**<br>I really don't feel like studying for this ol' science test. |
| ZACHARY turns to look at the picture at the head of his bed. | I'd much rather look at my picture of Betty. She's so *beauuutiful.* Besides, I know an easier way to get an A than studying. |

14

ZACHARY straightens up when he hears his MOM from offstage.

**MOM'S VOICE**
Zachary, time for bed! Don't forget your prayers.

ZACHARY positions himself by his bed. He bows his head for prayer.

**ZACHARY**
Now I lay me down to rest.
Let Betty see that I'm the best.
And if there's just one thing I seek,
It's a kiss from her upon my cheek.

ZACHARY gets up, remembers another prayer, kneels, and bows head again.

Now I lay me down to sleep.
Don't let the teacher see me cheat.
If she does and takes my paper,
Help me somehow to escape her.

ZACHARY lies down on the bed, sighs, and then snores his way to dreamland.

Ahhh...Zzzzz...

**Puppeteers prepare for scene change.**

## SCENE 2: The Playground

 **Play track 3 on CD A.**

ZACHARY enters from stage right, carrying an unwrapped granola bar.

BETTY enters from stage left, carrying a lunch bag.

ZACHARY sees BETTY and stands at attention. (Italicized lines are unspoken thoughts so no lip-sync.)

**ZACHARY**
*(Unspoken) There's Betty. She's coming this way. She's coming right at me!*

BETTY walks closer to ZACHARY. ZACHARY moves around excitedly as his heartbeat gets louder and louder.

BETTY greets ZACHARY.

**BETTY**
Hi, Zachary. May I eat lunch with you?

| | |
|---|---|
| ZACHARY looks out at the audience. | **ZACHARY**<br>*(Unspoken) Is she talking to me?* |
| Then he looks at BETTY. | *(Spoken)* S-s-s-sure. |
| BETTY bows her head to pray. | **BETTY**<br>*(Unspoken) God is great; God is good.*<br>*Lord, I thank you for my food.*<br>*Let me be thankful with each bite,*<br>*Be more like you, and do what's right.*<br><br>*(Spoken)* Amen. |
| ZACHARY starts to take a bite. BETTY looks at him. | Aren't you going to pray first, Zachary? |
| ZACHARY looks around to see who's looking. | **ZACHARY**<br>*(Unspoken) Right here in front of everybody?*<br><br>*(Spoken)* Oh, yeah...sure. |
| ZACHARY bows head and prays quickly. | *(Unspoken) God is great; God is good.*<br>*Make my mom to send more food.*<br>*Have her run out of whole wheat bread,*<br>*And put more cookies in instead.*<br><br>*(Spoken)* Amen. |
| ZACHARY starts to take a bite but stops as BETTY begins talking. | **BETTY**<br>Isn't it awesome, Zachary, that we can talk to Jesus no matter where we are? |
| | **ZACHARY**<br>Huh? I mean, yeah, I guess so. |
| | **BETTY**<br>I think it's really neat the way God hears and answers our prayers. |
| ZACHARY leans closer and shows interest in what she's saying. | **ZACHARY**<br>Do you think God hears all of our prayers? |

| | |
|---|---|
| BETTY nods her head "yes." | **BETTY**<br>Yes, I do. |
| | **ZACHARY**<br>Really? All of them? |
| BETTY nods her head again. | **BETTY**<br>I'm sure of it. |
| | **ZACHARY**<br>(**Clears throat loudly**) Well, do you think God answers *all* of our prayers? |
| BETTY nods her head. | **BETTY**<br>Sure I do. |
| | **ZACHARY**<br>You mean God always gives us everything we ask for? |
| BETTY shakes her head "no." | **BETTY**<br>No, not that. My mom says that God always answers our prayers but that he doesn't always say "yes." |
| ZACHARY tilts his head to the side. | **ZACHARY**<br>What do you mean? |
| | **BETTY**<br>Well, does your mom always say "yes" when you ask her for ice cream? |
| ZACHARY jumps up and down. | **ZACHARY**<br>I wish! |
| | **BETTY**<br>What does she say? |
| ZACHARY nods his head "yes" and then shakes his head "no." | **ZACHARY**<br>Well, sometimes she says "yes," and sometimes she says "no." |

| | **BETTY** |
|---|---|
| BETTY moves closer to ZACHARY. | Uh-huh, and what does she say if it's almost time for dinner? |
| | **ZACHARY** |
| ZACHARY holds out a hand motioning to "wait." | She tells me to wait until after dinner. |
| | **BETTY** |
| | Yes, and even though God always hears our prayers and always answers, God doesn't always say "yes." |
| | **ZACHARY** |
| ZACHARY paces back and forth as if trying to get the lesson right. | So, if I ask God for something, he always hears me, but God may tell me "no," or God may tell me to wait. |
| | **BETTY** |
| | Or God may say "yes." |
| | **ZACHARY** |
| ZACHARY looks down. | What if we sort of accidentally pray for the wrong thing? What then? |
| | **BETTY** |
| BETTY puts her arm around ZACHARY's shoulders. | Well, I guess we should take prayer seriously. God is good, and we can always trust God to do what's best. I guess that's why sometimes the answer has to be "no." |
| | **ZACHARY** |
| | Boy, I'm gonna be more careful what I pray for. |
| | **BETTY** |
| | Really? What have you been praying for? |
| | **ZACHARY** |
| ZACHARY stammers as his heart beats louder and louder. ZACHARY moves slightly away from BETTY. | Well, I uh... |

**18**

| | |
|---|---|
| BETTY walks closer to ZACHARY as he backs away from her. | **BETTY**<br>Is it personal? |
| | **ZACHARY**<br>Yeah, I guess you could say that. |
| BETTY continues to walk closer to ZACHARY as he backs away from her. | |
| | **BETTY**<br>Oh, I'm sorry. Let's change the subject, OK? |
| BETTY stops, and ZACHARY relaxes. | |
| | **ZACHARY**<br>*(Unspoken) Boy, is it ever OK!* |
| ZACHARY looks at the audience and doesn't lip-sync the italicized words. | |
| ZACHARY looks at BETTY and speaks. | **(Spoken)** OK. Did you pray about our science test, Betty? |
| | **BETTY**<br>Yes, did you? |
| ZACHARY wiggles to show discomfort. | **ZACHARY**<br>Sort of. What was your prayer like? |
| | **BETTY**<br>I'll pray it for both of us, if you like. |
| | **ZACHARY**<br>Sure, I can use all the help I can get! |
| ZACHARY and BETTY bow their heads to pray. | **BETTY**<br>Dear Jesus,<br>Soon we must take our science test.<br>Help us to do our very best.<br>Let everything we say and do<br>Bring honor, Lord, to only you. |
| | **ZACHARY and BETTY**<br>Amen. |
| BETTY turns to ZACHARY. | **BETTY**<br>What was your prayer like, Zachary? |

ZACHARY wiggles uncomfortably as his heart begins to race.

BETTY and ZACHARY bow their heads.

BETTY jumps up and kisses ZACHARY on the cheek.

BETTY exits. ZACHARY faints.

## ZACHARY
I think maybe I need to redo mine. Do you mind if I pray right now?

## BETTY
No, not at all. Please do.

## ZACHARY
Dear Jesus,
I'm sorry, Lord, for planning to cheat.
And that my studying was incomplete.
Help me, even though I'm not ready. And thank you, Lord, for my friend Betty.
Amen.

## BETTY
Oh, Zachary, you're the best!

**THE END!**

# Wake Up, Sam!

**Topic:** God's Direction
**Scripture You Might Read:** 1 Samuel 3

**Scene:** Eli's bedroom

**Characters**
**ELI:** a man who helps young Samuel listen to God
**SAMUEL:** a boy who heeds Eli's advice and discovers that God directs us
**GOD'S VOICE:** heard offstage

**Teacher Tip** Make simple Bible costumes for your puppets by draping fabric over their shoulders or by using bandannas or handkerchiefs for headpieces. Tie a shoestring or piece of yarn around each puppet's head to secure the headpiece.

**Props:** You'll need two pillows, two safety pins, two Bible costumes, the bedroom background (p. 7), and two poster-board signs attached to sticks: One sign says "Zzzz," and the other sign says, "Samuel!"

**Setup:** Use the safety pins to attach the pillows to either side of the puppet stage foreground. Dress puppets in Bible costumes. Give the signs to two puppeteers, and have them sit backstage. Make a beard for Eli out of cotton balls or unraveled strips of gray yarn glued to paper.

Before the skit, divide the audience in half. Tell them that, when they see the "Zzzz" sign above Eli's head, one half of the audience will snore for Eli. Explain that the other half of the audience will snore for Samuel when they see the "Zzzz" sign over his head. When they see the "Samuel!" sign, the entire audience will call out his name. Have a quick practice, then on with the show!

## SCRIPT

| ACTIONS | WORDS |
| --- | --- |
|  ***Play track 4 on CD A.*** | |
| ELI enters from stage right, stretches, and yawns. He lies down on a pillow, covers his eyes with his arm, and goes to sleep. | **ELI**<br>Zzzz... |
| ***"Zzzz" sign enters over ELI's head, and the audience responds. Sign exits.*** | |
| SAMUEL enters from stage left, stretches and yawns, then lies down on the other | **SAMUEL**<br>Zzzz... |

pillow. He tosses and turns for a few seconds and then goes to sleep.

*"Zzzz" sign enters over SAMUEL's head, and the audience responds. Sign exits.*

*"Samuel!" sign enters, and the audience responds. Sign exits.*

SAMUEL rises and goes to ELI.

**SAMUEL**
Here I am. What do you want?

ELI rises.

**ELI**
What? I didn't call you. Go back to bed.

ELI and SAMUEL return to bed.

*"Zzzz" sign enters over ELI's head, and the audience responds. Sign exits.*

**ELI and SAMUEL**
Zzzz...

*"Zzzz" sign enters over SAMUEL's head, and the audience responds. Sign exits.*

*(Repeat two times.)*

*"Samuel!" sign enters, and the audience responds. Sign exits.*

SAMUEL pops up and looks around. He goes to ELI.

**SAMUEL**
Yes, what do you want?

ELI wakes up.

**ELI**
Sam, I want to get some sleep. Please go back to bed.

ELI lies down. SAMUEL returns to his bed.

**ELI and SAMUEL**
Zzzz...

*"Zzzz" sign enters over ELI's head, and the audience responds. Sign exits.*

*"Zzzz" sign enters over SAMUEL's head, and the audience responds. Sign exits.*

**22**

*(Repeat two times.)*

*"Samuel!" sign enters, and the audience responds. Sign exits.*

SAMUEL rises and goes to ELI.


ELI rises.

## SAMUEL
Here I am, Eli. Why do you keep calling me?

## ELI
Sam, I'm not calling you. Do you have any idea what time it is?

## SAMUEL
But I'm sure I heard you calling my name. I heard you say, "Samuel."

## ELI
It wasn't me, but I think maybe I know who it was. Sammy, you go back to bed. When you hear your name called, say, "Speak, for your servant is listening." It's the Lord who's trying to get your attention.

ELI lies down and goes to sleep.

SAMUEL returns to bed but tosses and turns, thinking he hears something. Finally, he settles back down and goes to sleep.

*"Zzzz" sign enters over ELI's head, and the audience responds. Sign exits.*

*"Zzzz" sign enters over SAMUEL's head and the audience responds. Sign exits.*

*(Repeat two times.)*

*"Samuel!" sign enters, and the audience responds. Sign exits.*

## ELI and SAMUEL
Zzzz...

SAMUEL sits up.

**SAMUEL**
Is that you, Lord? I'm all ears! No, wait a minute...Speak, for your servant is listening!

**GOD'S VOICE**
I'm about to do something in Israel that will make everyone's ears tingle. You will be my prophet and tell people about me. You will listen to me, and I will direct you.

SAMUEL lies down and tries to go back to sleep. He tosses and turns and then finally quiets down.

**SAMUEL**
Wow...Listen to God...God will direct me...

*"Zzzz" sign enters over ELI's head, and the audience responds. Sign exits.*

**ELI and SAMUEL**
Zzzz...

*"Zzzz" sign enters over SAMUEL's head, and the audience responds. Sign exits.*

*(Repeat two times.)*

ELI awakens suddenly.

**ELI**
I wonder what the Lord told Samuel. Samuel! Samuel!

SAMUEL pops up, thinking it's the Lord speaking.

**SAMUEL**
I'm ready, Lord. Lay it on me!

Oh, it's just you!

ELI walks over to SAMUEL.

**ELI**
Excuse me?

**SAMUEL**
Oh, nothing. It's just that the Lord spoke to me last night, and I was hoping it would be him again.

**ELI**
Well, out with it boy! What did God say to you?

SAMUEL's mouth hangs open with awe.

**SAMUEL**

It was pretty awesome.

**ELI**

Come now, don't hold back! Give me every detail.

**SAMUEL**

God told me that he was going to do something in Israel. Everyone's ears will tingle when they hear of it.

**ELI**

What the Lord said is right. Let God do what he sees as good.

ELI exits stage right.

SAMUEL bows his head.

**GOD'S VOICE**

I was with Samuel and directed him as he grew up—and as long as he lived. People listened to all Samuel said, and they knew he spoke for me.

SAMUEL exits stage left.

**THE END!**

# Don't Climb the Tree!

**Topic:** God's Way
**Scriptures You Might Read:** 1 Samuel 8; 9:1-2; 10:17-24; 2 Peter 3:9b

**Scene:** Outside by a large tree

## Characters
**GRIZZLE:** a rugged, tough outdoorsman
**PERCIVAL:** a precise, dapper gentleman

**Teacher Tip** Make 3-D leaves for the tree out of various colors of construction paper, folding each leaf lengthwise and taping it to the tree. Make it look as if Percival is climbing the tree all by himself by sticking a long dowel inside the puppet and raising the dowel from behind the puppet stage and behind the tree.

**Props:** You'll need sports clothes and a tie for the puppets and two poster-board signs attached to sticks: One says, "Don't climb the tree!" and the other says, "God knows best!"

**Setup:** Dress Grizzle in sports clothes (baseball cap turned backward) or outdoors clothes (scarf wrapped around neck or orange vest). Dress Percival in a tie. Use poster board to create a large tree in the center of the foreground. Give the signs to two puppeteers, and have them sit backstage.

Before the skit, practice shouting the words on the two signs with the audience.

## SCRIPT

| ACTIONS | WORDS |
|---|---|
|  **Play track 5 on CD A.** | |
| PERCIVAL enters from stage right, spies the tree, and walks over to admire it. PERCIVAL walks with short, precise movements. | **PERCIVAL** <br> What a magnificent specimen of a tree! |
| GRIZZLE enters from stage right and joins PERCIVAL. GRIZZLE walks with big, bold steps. | **GRIZZLE** <br> Hey, bud! Whatcha' doin'? |
| PERCIVAL turns to GRIZZLE and extends his hand for a handshake. | **PERCIVAL** <br> Hello, my name is Percival Alexander Veryimportant, the Third. And to whom am I speaking? |

GRIZZLE looks at PERCIVAL's outstretched hand and tries to give him a high five but fails.

**GRIZZLE**
Howdy, Pers! I'm Grizzle! But you can call me Griz.

**PERCIVAL**
Pleased to make your acquaintance, I'm sure...er...Mr. Griz.

GRIZZLE nods head.

**GRIZZLE**
Yeah, I'm sure you are, too. So, what's up?

PERCIVAL looks up at the tree.

**PERCIVAL**
Actually, I've been standing here admiring this mighty Quercus alba.

GRIZZLE shakes his head in a double take.

**GRIZZLE**
Say what?

PERCIVAL points to the tree.

**PERCIVAL**
Oh, I do beg your pardon. I've just been standing here admiring this stately white oak.

GRIZZLE walks around to the other side of the tree.

**GRIZZLE**
You mean this tree?

PERCIVAL looks the tree up and down.

**PERCIVAL**
Quite right, Mr. Griz. Isn't it majestic in form and graceful in stature?

GRIZZLE moves closer to the tree and looks it up and down.

**GRIZZLE**
Looks like a plain old tree to me.

**PERCIVAL**
It's far from a plain old tree, Mr. Griz. Why, this tree has probably been standing here for one hundred years or more. Who knows, it may have been there when our forefathers founded this country.

| | |
|---|---|
| GRIZZLE scratches his head in amazement. | **GRIZZLE**<br>Well, ya don't say? All I know, Pers old pal, is that it's been here ever since I was a kid. Why, I remember my buddies and I used to go right up to the top of this tree. |
| PERCIVAL looks at the top of the tree and then at GRIZZLE. | **PERCIVAL**<br>Indeed? |
| GRIZZLE points to PERCIVAL and then to the tree. | **GRIZZLE**<br>Sure, lots of times! Say, it sounds like you've never even climbed a tree. |
| | **PERCIVAL**<br>I have never felt the need to leave the ground, Mr. Griz. |
| | **GRIZZLE**<br>Oh, so you're scared, aren't ya? |
| PERCIVAL looks up at the top of the tree and then points to the ground. | **PERCIVAL**<br>Why, no, of course not! I just think that the perspective is so much lovelier from down here. |
| GRIZZLE nods his head "yes." | **GRIZZLE**<br>Yep! I thought so! |
| PERCIVAL turns to GRIZZLE. | **PERCIVAL**<br>Excuse me? |
| GRIZZLE leans around the tree toward PERCIVAL. | **GRIZZLE**<br>Well, never mind. You don't have to climb the tree if you're *too scared*. |
| PERCIVAL shakes in fright. | **PERCIVAL**<br>Too scared? Too scared? I am certainly not scared! |
| | **GRIZZLE**<br>Then why are you shaking? |

| | |
|---|---|
| PERCIVAL turns his back on GRIZZLE. | **PERCIVAL**<br>I said, "I am not scared!" |
| GRIZZLE points to the top of the tree. | **GRIZZLE**<br>Well, then prove it. Let's see you climb all the way to the top! |
| PERCIVAL looks up to the top and shakes in fear. | **PERCIVAL**<br>All, all, all the way to the t-t-t-t-top? |
| GRIZZLE looks up to the top of the tree and then at PERCIVAL. | **GRIZZLE**<br>Yep, right up to the tippy top. But you won't make it, Mr. Percival, 'cause you're afraid! |
| PERCIVAL stops shaking and stands straight. | **PERCIVAL**<br>OK! OK! I'll do it! But, but, but first I have to pray. I always pray before starting any new endeavor. |
| GRIZZLE nods his head "yes." | **GRIZZLE**<br>Yeah, you better pray 'cause you're gonna need all the help you can get. |
| PERCIVAL bows his head and puts his hands together in a silent prayer. | |
| **"Don't climb the tree!" sign appears, and the audience responds. Sign exits.** | |
| GRIZZLE appears not to hear anything. PERCIVAL looks up toward heaven when children respond and then turns to GRIZZLE. | **PERCIVAL**<br>I'm sorry, Mr. Griz, but I think God is telling me not to climb the tree. |
| | **GRIZZLE**<br>Oh, so now you're using God as your excuse not to climb the tree. |
| | **PERCIVAL**<br>Well, well, well, it's just th-th-that... |
| **"Don't climb the tree!" sign appears, and the audience responds. Sign exits.** | |

29

PERCIVAL looks up to heaven when children respond to sign.

GRIZZLE looks like he doesn't hear anything.

**GRIZZLE**
It's just that you're a chicken!

PERCIVAL stands straight and tall and then points to the tree.

**PERCIVAL**
Now stop that this instant! I will simply not be provoked into climbing that tree.

***"Don't climb the tree!" sign appears, and the audience responds. Sign exits.***

GRIZZLE looks like he doesn't hear anything.

PERCIVAL looks up to heaven when children respond to sign.

GRIZZLE moves his head forward and back, like a chicken.

**GRIZZLE**
(Makes chicken sounds.)

PERCIVAL shakes with anger.

**PERCIVAL**
Oooooooh! I'll show you who's a chicken!

PERCIVAL climbs the tree from behind. The tree shakes to indicate PERCIVAL is climbing.

Oh, my! I made it! The view is so panoramic from way up here. Just look over there!

GRIZZLE doesn't take his eyes off the top of the tree.

**GRIZZLE**
Pers, Pers...Be careful, buddy. I didn't mean for you to...Hey, don't let go!

PERCIVAL falls from the tree with a big thud and lies on the ground on his back.

**PERCIVAL**
Oof! Ow! Ouch! Owie!

GRIZZLE runs over to PERCIVAL and stares down at him.

**GRIZZLE**
Are you OK? Pers...Pers, speak to me! Are you hurt?

PERCIVAL lifts his head slightly and makes sickly chicken sounds.

**PERCIVAL**
(Makes chicken sounds.)

GRIZZLE has compassion for PERCIVAL.

PERCIVAL lifts his head.

GRIZZLE helps PERCIVAL offstage.

**"God knows best!" sign appears, and the audience responds. Sign exits.**

## GRIZZLE
Oh, Percival! I'm so sorry.

## PERCIVAL
I knew I should have listened to God. Ooooooooo!

**THE END!**

# Silly Friends

**Topic:** Friendship

**Scriptures You Might Read:** 1 Samuel 18:1-4; 19:1-7; 20; Proverbs 18:24b

**Scene:** Your meeting area

## Characters

**BILLY:** a boy who misses his friend
**SILLY:** a boy who wants to be a friend
**LEADER:** interacts with puppets and audience

**Props:** No extra props are needed.

**Setup:** Practice the skit with the puppets and the CD to get the timing down.

........................ **SCRIPT** ........................

| ACTIONS | WORDS |
|---|---|
|  **Play track 6 on CD A.**<br><br>LEADER enters, stands in front of the puppet stage, and then speaks to the audience. | **LEADER**<br>Hi, everyone! Today we're going to talk about friends. Raise your hand if you have a best friend. |
| Pause for children to respond. | Wow! That's a lot of best friends! Tell the person next to you what you like about your best friend? |
| Pause for children to respond.<br><br>BILLY enters the stage and interrupts. | **BILLY**<br>Ahem. Ahem! *Ahem!* |
| LEADER turns to BILLY when speaking to him and turns to the audience when speaking to them. | **LEADER**<br>Oh! Hi there, Billy! Kids, this is Billy. Billy just moved into town. Billy, these are the boys and girls. |

| | |
|---|---|
| BILLY hangs his head sadly. | **BILLY**<br>(**Sadly**) Oh, hello. Did I hear you talking about best friends? |
| | **LEADER**<br>Yes, Billy. I was asking these guys what they like about their best friends. |
| | **BILLY**<br>I had a best friend. |
| SILLY enters the stage, bouncing excitedly and bumping into BILLY. | **SILLY**<br>Best friend? Best friend? Did someone say best friend. |
| BILLY rubs arm and moves away from SILLY. | |
| LEADER moves over to BILLY and pats his back. | **LEADER**<br>Silly, please be careful. I think you need to say something. |
| SILLY turns to LEADER and moves his head from side to side, acting confused. | **SILLY**<br>I do? |
| | **LEADER**<br>Yes, you do. |
| SILLY looks up at the ceiling and then all around while thinking. Then SILLY looks at the LEADER while he asks the question. | **SILLY**<br>Umm...ah...What am I supposed to say? |
| LEADER points to BILLY. | **LEADER**<br>Well, for starters, you could apologize for bumping into Billy. |
| SILLY bounces over to BILLY and slugs BILLY on the arm when he says, "Sorry!" | **SILLY**<br>Oh, yeah! Sorry! |
| BILLY rubs his arm and backs away. | **BILLY**<br>Oof! That's OK, I guess. |

SILLY energetically bounces up and down and then looks at the LEADER.

**SILLY**
Anything else?

LEADER motions to BILLY and to the audience.

**LEADER**
You could introduce yourself to Billy and to the children.

SILLY acts really excited, bouncing all around while talking to the audience.

**SILLY**
Hi, guys! I'm Silly! Well, I'm not *silly*. I mean I am *Silly* but not really...Oh, you know what I mean.

LEADER chuckles and then faces SILLY.

**LEADER**
You mean, your *name* is Silly.

SILLY nods his head excitedly.

**SILLY**
Yeah! That's what I said! I'm Silly!

BILLY walks slowly a little closer to SILLY, trying to get everyone's attention again.

**BILLY**
Ahem. Ahem! *Ahem!*

SILLY looks at BILLY and then points at BILLY when speaking.

**SILLY**
Hey, what's his problem? Does he have a sore throat?

**LEADER**
No, Silly. I believe Billy was going to tell us all about his best friend.

SILLY gets excited again and begins bouncing.

**SILLY**
Best friend? Best friend? I've always wanted to be a best friend!

LEADER takes hold of SILLY to calm him down and then turns to BILLY.

**LEADER**
Silly, please, calm down. Go ahead, Billy. Tell us about your best friend.

BILLY hangs his head and wipes his eyes as if wiping away tears.

**BILLY**
Before I moved here, I had a best friend.

**34**

| | |
|---|---|
| LEADER continues holding SILLY, who squirms. | **LEADER**<br>What did you and your best friend like to do? |
| BILLY stands a little straighter. | **BILLY**<br>Well, we liked to play soccer. My best friend is the best goalie where I used to live. |
| SILLY breaks free from the LEADER and bounces up and down. He's excited again. | **SILLY**<br>Soccer? Soccer? I love to play soccer. I could be a best friend. One! Two! Three strikes! You're out! Batter up! |
| BILLY holds a hand over his mouth and tries not to laugh. | **BILLY**<br>That's not soccer, Silly. That's baseball. |
| SILLY calms down slightly. | **SILLY**<br>Oh, well! If I had someone to teach me, I could play soccer, too. |
| LEADER turns to the audience. ***Stop the CD while children respond, then play track 7 on CD A.*** | **LEADER**<br>Friends can help us learn all kinds of things like playing sports, reading or doing math at school, or learning about Jesus at church. Kids, what are some of the things your friends help you learn? |
| BILLY hangs his head sadly again because he misses his friend. | **BILLY**<br>My best friend was a really good listener. |
| SILLY gets excited and bounces and holds his hand up to his mouth for "Shh!" | **SILLY**<br>Listener? Listener? SHH! SHH! SHH! I'm a great listener! I said, "SHH!" Did you hear me?! I could be a best friend! |
| BILLY laughs at SILLY's antics. | **BILLY**<br>Listening doesn't mean to tell others to shush, Silly. |

SILLY calms down slightly.

**SILLY**

Well, if someone talked to me the way you do, Billy, I could be a great listener.

**Stop the CD,** and ask the audience the two questions.

**LEADER**

Having a friend who listens is very important. Kids, can I see by a show of hands how many of you have friends who are good listeners?

Pause for children to respond.

How many of *you* are good listeners?

Pause for children to respond, **then play track 8 on CD A.**

BILLY wipes away tears.

**BILLY**

I miss my best friend.

SILLY wipes away a tear in sympathy for BILLY. He pats BILLY on the back gently.

**SILLY**

Me, too.

BILLY stands straighter and wiggles with laughter.

**BILLY**

But you don't even know him.

SILLY gets excited again.

**SILLY**

Oh! Oh! Yeah! That's right! I forgot! Well, I guess I can miss *being* a best friend.

LEADER turns to BILLY and speaks gently.

**LEADER**

Billy, have you talked to God about how you feel? God is always with us whenever we need a friend.

BILLY nods his head.

**BILLY**

Yeah, I told God how much I miss my friend.

SILLY is really, really excited.

**SILLY**

Talk to God? Talk to God? I just talked to God this morning. Wanna know what God said?

**36**

| | |
|---|---|
| BILLY turns to SILLY, leans closer, and is interested in what he has to say. | **BILLY**<br>Yeah! What did God say? |
| SILLY is calm. | **SILLY**<br>God said I could be a best friend. |
| | **LEADER**<br>I think God has provided a best friend for both of you. |
| BILLY wiggles with laughter. | **BILLY**<br>You make me laugh, Silly. I never had a friend that could make me laugh the way you do. |
| SILLY opens mouth in amazement. | **SILLY**<br>Friend? You called me *friend?* |
| BILLY pats SILLY on the back. | **BILLY**<br>Come on, Silly. I'll teach you how to play soccer. |
| SILLY bounces around, really excited again. | **SILLY**<br>Soccer? Soccer? Great! Can you show me how to slam-dunk the ball? |
| BILLY nods his head and answers as they exit. | **BILLY**<br>Sure, Silly. |

**THE END!**

SKIT FOUR: SILLY FRIENDS

# Really Able

**Topic:** Reliability
**Scriptures You Might Read:** 2 Samuel 5:1-5; Psalm 37; 46:1

**Scene:** Outside the classroom

**Characters**
**JIM:** a boy who missed a word on his spelling test
**JAM:** a girl who missed the same word

> **Teacher Tip** Instead of using a small, lightweight book for the dictionary, make one by folding a red sheet of construction paper in half. Use a black marker to write the word "Dictionary" across one side of it.

**Props:** You'll need two papers for spelling tests; a small, lightweight book for a dictionary; and five poster-board signs on sticks: "R-E *L-I* A-B-L-E" "*R-E-L-I...A-B-L-E*" "Yep!" "Nope!" and "God is *RELIABLE*! You can count on him!"

**Setup:** Attach a sheet of paper to one hand on each puppet. Have the dictionary backstage ready to be attached to Jam's hand later in the skit. Give the signs to two puppeteers, and have them sit backstage.

Before the skit, practice with the audience shouting the words to the signs that say "Yep!" "Nope!" and "God is *RELIABLE*! You can count on him!" Tell them not to respond to the spelling signs.

## SCRIPT

| ACTIONS | WORDS |
|---|---|
|  **Play track 9 on CD A.** | |
| JIM enters stage right, looking at the paper attached to his hand. | **JIM** I thought I got 100 percent on the spelling test, but it looks like I missed one. **(Sighs)** Oh, well. No big deal. |
| JAM enters from stage left, looking at the paper attached to her hand. JAM walks over to JIM. | **JAM** Hi, Jim! What's up? |
| JIM holds up his paper. | **JIM** Hey, Jam! Nothing much; just looking over this old spelling test. |
| | **JAM** How did you do? |

**38**

| | **JIM** |
| JIM looks at his paper. | Not too bad. I only missed one. |
| | |
| | **JAM** |
| JAM holds up her paper. | Me, too. Have you looked up the definition yet? |
| | |
| | **JIM** |
| JIM shakes head "no." | No, that's a pain. Every time we miss a spelling word, Miss Hootenheimer makes us look up the definition. |
| | |
| | **JAM** |
| | Yeah, it sure is a pain. Why do we have to understand the meaning of a word to know how to spell it? |
| | |
| | **JIM** |
| | You got me. It must be a teacher thing. |
| | |
| | **JAM** |
| JAM looks down at her paper. | Oh, well. I think I know the meaning of the word I missed. |
| | |
| | **JIM** |
| JIM looks at his paper. | I think I may know the meaning of my word, too. But something doesn't seem right. |
| | |
| JIM shakes his head. | |
| | |
| JAM tries to look at JIM's paper. | **JAM** |
| | Really? Which word did you miss? |
| | |
| | **JIM** |
| JIM shows JAM his paper. | This one. |
| | |
| | **JAM** |
| JAM holds up her paper. | Hey! That's the same word I missed! |
| | |
| | **JIM** |
| | And you think you know the meaning? |

| | |
|---|---|
| JAM nods her head "yes." | **JAM**<br>Yep, it's easy! |
| JIM studies his paper and scratches his head. | **JIM**<br>Easy? But it doesn't make sense. |
| | **JAM**<br>Why? |
| | **JIM**<br>I heard Pastor Rusty say that God was like this. |
| | **JAM**<br>Yeah, so? |
| | **JIM**<br>So? But God wouldn't be like that! |
| JAM nods her head "yes." | **JAM**<br>Sure, God is! |
| JIM vigorously shakes his head "no." | **JIM**<br>Are you crazy? No way! |
| | **JAM**<br>You mean you don't believe God is like that? |
| JIM shakes his head "no." | **JIM**<br>Of course not! God wouldn't fib! |
| JAM does a double take. | **JAM**<br>Everybody knows that God wouldn't fib. |
| JIM points to his paper. | **JIM**<br>So how does this word describe God? |
| | **JAM**<br>Because God really can do it! |

SKIT FIVE: REALLY ABLE

**JIM**
But God is truth, so God wouldn't do it!

JAM raises her hands in frustration.

**JAM**
Do what?!

**JIM**
Tell lies over and over again.

JAM shakes her head.

**JAM**
And you called *me* crazy?

JIM shakes his paper in front of her.

**JIM**
Well, that's what the spelling word means!

**"R-E-L-I...A-B-L-E" sign appears and
remains.**

**JAM**
What are you talking about? The spelling
word is "reliable" or "really able." R-E-L-I...
A-B-L-E. And after all, God is really, really,
really able.

**"R-E L-I A-B-L-E" sign appears, and
both signs remain.**

**JIM**
Really able?! No! "Reliable"...R-E *L-I* A-B-L-E!
It means to tell lies over and over again. And
God would never do that. God would never
even tell one lie.

**JAM**
It's "*really able*"! That means that God can do
anything!

JIM waves his paper overhead.

**JIM**
No, it's "re *lie* able"! It means fibbing all the
time.

**41**

| | |
|---|---|
| JAM shouts. | **JAM**<br>No, it's not! |
| JIM gets in JAM's face. | **JIM**<br>Yes, it is! |
| They stare each other down until JAM finally speaks. | |
| JAM points to the audience. | **JAM**<br>Why don't we ask them? |
| JIM turns to audience. | **JIM**<br>OK, OK! Hey, everyone! Is the word spelled r-e-l-i-a-b-l-e? |
| ***"Yep!" sign appears, and the audience responds. Sign exits.*** | |
| JIM turns to JAM. | See? "Reliable" means to tell lies again and again. |
| ***"Nope!" sign appears, and the audience responds. Sign exits.*** | |
| JAM turns to JIM and then turns to the audience. | **JAM**<br>I told you! See, "reliable" means really able! Doesn't it? |
| ***"Nope!" sign appears, and the audience responds. Sign exits.*** | |
| JIM and JAM look at each other. | **JIM and JAM**<br>Huh? |
| | **JIM**<br>Maybe we should look it up in the dictionary. |
| | **JAM**<br>OK, I'll be right back. |

SKIT FIVE: REALLY ABLE

JAM exits stage left.

While a dictionary is being attached to JAM's hand, JIM is looking confused and mumbling on stage.

JAM returns, looking at the dictionary attached to her hand.

JIM looks at the dictionary too.

JAM looks down at the book and then looks at JIM.

JIM looks up at the audience.

JAM looks back in the book.

JIM nods his head "yes."

**JIM and JAM both exit as "God is RELIABLE! You can count on him!" sign appears, and the audience responds. Sign exits.**

**JIM**
"Yep," "Nope," "Yep," "Nope"...Well, what is it? What does "reliable" mean? I'm soooo confused.

What does it say?

**JAM**
You were right. It's pronounced re-*li*-able.

**JIM**
Well, I thought so. So what does it mean?

**JAM**
It means to be able to count on someone.

**JIM**
Now that makes sense because we can always count on God! God always knows what's best for us. God never lets us down.

**JAM**
Well, if that's what reliable means, then God is really reliable. Aren't you glad we didn't miss the word *antidisestablishmentarianism*?

**THE END!**

# Powerful Words

**Topic:** Repentance
**Scriptures You Might Read:** 2 Samuel 11; 12:1-10; Psalm 51:1-12; Colossians 3:13

**Scene 1:** A living room
**Scene 2:** A park

## Characters
**BETH:** an eight-year-old girl who's celebrating her birthday
**MARK:** Beth's sixteen-year-old brother
**LEADER:** interacts with audience
**KIM'S VOICE:** heard offstage
**PETE'S VOICE:** heard offstage

**Props:** You'll need a party noisemaker, a gift bow, a Bible, the living room background (p. 9), and a poster-board sign on a stick that says, "Say you're sorry."

**Setup:** Give the noisemaker to the leader. Have puppeteers backstage ready to attach a gift bow to Mark, hold the sign on cue, and make a quick scene change to the in-line skating park.

Before the skit, practice reading the sign on cue with the audience.

SCRIPT

| ACTIONS | WORDS |
| --- | --- |
| LEADER enters, stands in front of the puppet stage, and sounds the party noisemaker to get kids' attention. | **LEADER**<br>The skit we'll see today is about Beth, who just turned eight years old. Beth gets to go in-line skating with her friends. Before we see the skit, I was wondering what you like to do with your friends? |
| Pause for children to respond. | OK, now raise your hand if you've ever had a fight with a friend and had to say you were sorry. |

44

Pause for children to respond.

Everyone has to say sorry sometimes, right? Our skit is called, "Powerful Words." Beth is about to learn more about the powerful words, "I'm sorry." Let's sing "Happy Birthday" and let Beth know we're here!

LEADER directs children in singing "Happy Birthday" as BETH and MARK enter from stage right. Play the party noisemaker as children sing.

## SCENE 1: The Birthday Girl's Living Room

 **Play track 10 on CD A.**

BETH speaks to the children in the audience.

## BETH

I'm eight years old today, and I got my very own in-line skates! Can you believe that?

MARK and BETH look at each other.

## MARK

I have a present for you too. But you have to close your eyes first.

BETH closes her eyes by either bowing her head or covering her eyes with her hands. MARK dips below stage and a puppeteer puts a gift bow on MARK's forehead.

MARK appears again.

## BETH

Can I open my eyes yet?

## MARK

OK, open your eyes!

BETH opens her eyes and looks all around—anywhere but at MARK.

## BETH

Where's my present?

BETH continues looking around. MARK tries to get her attention by waving his arms.

| | |
|---|---|
| BETH looks at MARK, asks the question, does a double take, and then makes the statement to MARK. | **BETH**<br>I give up. Where's my present? Uh...Mark, don't look now, but there's a bow on your head. |
| | **MARK**<br>Yes! You know how you always want to come along when I go out with my friends? |
| BETH nods her head "yes." | Well, that's my present to you! I'm your present! |
| BETH jumps up and down with joy. | **BETH**<br>I get to hang out with my big brother? What a cool present! |
| MARK shakes his head "no." | **MARK**<br>No, no, that's not it. You're not going to hang out with my friends. I'm going to hang out with yours! |
| BETH tilts her head toward MARK. | **BETH**<br>What? You're going to pal around with me and my friends? |
| MARK shakes his head "no." | **MARK**<br>I'm going to take you and two of your friends to a park to use your new in-line skates. |
| BETH leans in toward MARK. | **BETH**<br>You're going to drive us? |
| | **MARK**<br>Yep. |
| BETH leans closer to MARK. | **BETH**<br>And hang out with us? |
| MARK points to the bow on his head. | **MARK**<br>Yep. Here I am. |

| | **BETH** |
|---|---|
| BETH hugs MARK. | Oh, Mark, thank you! You're the best birthday present! When can we go? |
| | **MARK** |
| | We can go as soon as you think of two friends to invite. |
| BETH jumps up and down excitedly. | **BETH** |
| | Can I take Kim? She has in-line skates. |
| | **MARK** |
| | Sure, go call her. |
| BETH starts to leave to the left but turns back around. | **BETH** |
| | I can't invite Kim to come along. |
| | **MARK** |
| | Why not? |
| | **BETH** |
| | Because we're fighting. |
| | **MARK** |
| | About what? |
| BETH starts to pace back and forth. | **BETH** |
| | She's just being stubborn, and I'm right. Do you want to know what she did? Well, I'll tell ya. First, she... |
| BETH stops pacing. | **MARK** |
| | (**Interrupts**) I don't need to know what you're fighting about. Why don't you just tell her you're sorry so you two can be friends again? Then we can go in-line skating. |
| BETH shakes her head "no." | **BETH** |
| | No! |

**MARK**
Why not?

**BETH**
Because.

**MARK**
Because you're stubborn too?

BETH shakes her head vigorously.

**BETH**
I'm not stubborn, and I'm not going to apologize!

MARK shrugs.

**MARK**
Suit yourself, but people who don't apologize don't have many friends.

BETH starts to leave to the right. She's almost out of sight but then returns to MARK.

**BETH**
I have more friends. I don't need Kim. I'll invite Pete, our next-door neighbor, to come.

BETH looks at the audience and then at MARK.

Uh...Pete can't come.

**MARK**
How do you know? You haven't even asked him yet.

**BETH**
He's busy.

**MARK**
Let me guess...You're fighting.

BETH starts to pace back and forth.

**BETH**
Yes, but it wasn't my fault. He said I was...

BETH stops and looks at MARK.

**MARK**
(**Interrupts**) Stop right there! I don't need to know what happened. You just have to fix things with Pete, that's all.

**BETH**

But I can't. We're fighting, and he's wrong.

MARK puts his hand on BETH's back.

**MARK**

Well, Beth, it looks like we have a great outing planned, but no friends to share it with. Maybe I'd better think of another present—something you can do all by yourself because, after all, you're mad at everybody.

MARK points to the bow on his head and then moves as if to walk away.

BETH stops MARK.

**BETH**

Wait! I'll make some new friends!

**MARK**

Why don't you just fix things with your old friends?

**BETH**

How?

MARK holds out a hand for emphasis.

**MARK**

I told you, say you're sorry for whatever they think you've done wrong. They'll probably apologize for whatever they've done wrong too. Then everything will be fine.

**BETH**

What if they don't apologize?

**MARK**

Then at least you'll have the good feeling that you did what God wants you to do.

BETH tilts her head as she asks the question.

**BETH**

What God wants me to do? I'm mad at Pete and Kim; I'm not mad at God!

SKIT SIX: POWERFUL WORDS

MARK shakes head and then looks to the audience.

 **LEADER stops the CD** and helps someone find the verse. LEADER helps the child bring the Bible to MARK and hold it so it looks like he's reading. **Play track 11 on CD A.**

LEADER has the child sit down again.

BETH walks to stage left.

MARK follows her.

BETH looks up and then looks at MARK.

MARK puts his arm around BETH.

MARK exits.

BETH paces back and forth across the stage.

**"Say you're sorry!" sign appears, and the audience responds. Sign exits.**

## MARK
Let me show you something. Does someone have a Bible out there?

## MARK
Can you have the leader help you find Colossians 3:13 and then bring the Bible to me so I can read it?

In Colossians 3:13, God says, "Bear with each other and forgive whatever grievances you may have against one another. Forgive as the Lord forgave you."

Hey, thanks for holding the Bible for me!

## BETH
I don't see why it matters to God if I work things out with Pete and Kim.

## MARK
God wants us to care about our friends. It makes God sad when we hurt each other.

## BETH
Then I'll tell God I'm sorry for being mad at Pete and Kim.

## MARK
That's fine, but God also wants you to tell your friends you're sorry and make it better between you. You can do it. I know you can!

## BETH
I don't know what to say to Kim.

## BETH

**(To herself)** Say I'm sorry! Oh...I don't know. Maybe I should go to Pete first, but I don't know what to say to Pete.

*"Say you're sorry!" sign appears, and the audience responds. Sign exits.*

BETH faces the audience.

**(As though she came up with the idea herself)** Maybe I should say, "I'm sorry." OK! If that's what God wants me to do, I guess I'll do it.

BETH exits.

*Puppeteers change the background to the roller-blade park.*

## SCENE 2: The Park

 **Play track 12 on CD A.**

BETH enters from stage left, and MARK enters from stage right. They glide as if they're in-line skating. They meet center stage and look out at the audience. They both move their heads from stage left to stage right as if they're watching KIM skate by. They wave at KIM.

## KIM'S VOICE

**(Offstage)** Whee! This is great, Beth!

BETH continues to wave at KIM.

## BETH

You're doing great on your in-line skates, Kim!

BETH and MARK turn their heads at the same time, looking from stage right to stage left, as if they're watching PETE skate by. They wave at PETE.

## PETE'S VOICE

**(Offstage)** I am so cool! Whooooa!

BETH continues to wave at PETE.

## BETH

Great job, Pete! You're awesome!

BETH waves so enthusiastically that she bumps into MARK and almost knocks him over.

## BETH

Oh, I'm sorry. I'm still getting used to these skates. We're having a blast! Thanks for everything! You're the best present ever.

## MARK

No, you gave yourself your best present.

You gave yourself your friends back by saying you were sorry. You took God's advice.

BETH tilts her head as if puzzled.

## BETH

I guess I did, huh? We can tell God we're sorry when we do wrong, and he forgives us. And God wants us to tell others we're sorry when we hurt them, too. Cool!

BETH and MARK skate away together as she says her lines.

BETH and MARK exit offstage.

## ALL

(**Offstage**) Oh, I'm sorry.
I'm sorry I ran into you.
Oh, are you OK?
I'm so sorry. I'm not very coordinated on these things yet.
I'm soooooo sorry!
Please forgive me.

The audience hears from offstage KIM, PETE, BETH, and MARK crash together and tumble—using powerful words to apologize.

**THE END!**

# God Rules!

**Topic:** Choices
**Scriptures You Might Read:** 1 Kings 11:28-12:24; 2 Chronicles 7:14

**Scene 1:** The zoo tour
**Scene 2:** The cleanup

## Characters
**KAJA:** a little girl who wants to obey the rules
**KENDRA:** her friend who doesn't want to obey the rules
**LEADER:** interacts with the audience
**ZOO TOUR GUIDE:** heard offstage

**Props:** You'll need a wrapped piece of gum; two rags; a small bucket (optional); and pictures of a lion, elephant, cow, tropical bird, and monkey (pp. 10-12).

**Setup:** Enlarge and attach each animal picture to a stick. Give the props and the signs to puppeteers backstage.

Before the skit, practice making animal sounds with the audience for each of the animal signs you created.

---

### SCRIPT

| ACTIONS | WORDS |
|---|---|
| LEADER enters, stands in front of puppet stage, and welcomes the group. | **LEADER**<br>It's good to see everyone here today. The skit is called "God Rules," so let's start by talking about rules. What's a rule you have to follow at home or at school? |
| LEADER pauses after each question to get several answers from the children. | What's a rule that God wants you to follow? Why do we even have rules? What happens if you break a rule? |
|  | Rules help us know what to do and what not to do so we can live together peacefully. God gives us choices about whether or not to follow the rules. Let's see what happens in today's story when Kendra and her friend Kaja choose to break a rule at the zoo. |

## SCENE 1: The Zoo Tour

 *Play track 13 on CD A.*

KENDRA and KAJA enter the stage, looking all around.

**KAJA**
Stick close by me, Kendra. This zoo tour moves pretty fast, and I don't want us to get separated.

**ZOO TOUR GUIDE**
Everyone, please follow me.

KAJA and KENDRA cross the stage in a single-file line, disappear out of view, and then reappear right away, coming from the direction in which they disappeared, as though they were following the tour.

Today's tour begins at the lion cage.

*Picture of a lion appears, and the audience responds. Picture disappears.*

KENDRA and KAJA tremble.

**KENDRA**
Look at the size of those lions. They're so scary!

KENDRA and KAJA cross the stage, disappear again, and reappear instantly, as if following the tour.

**ZOO TOUR GUIDE**
The next exhibit shows our rare African bull elephants.

*Picture of an elephant appears, and the audience responds. Picture disappears.*

**KAJA**
I've never seen animals that big. They sure are loud!

KENDRA and KAJA cross the stage, disappear again, and reappear instantly, continuing their tour.

**54**

### ZOO TOUR GUIDE

Next we come to the petting-zoo cow exhibit. These are some of the finest cows from all over the world.

*Cow picture appears, and the audience responds. Picture disappears.*

### KAJA

Can you believe we get milk, cheese, yogurt, cream, and cottage cheese from those guys?

### KENDRA

Those aren't guys—those are girls. And don't forget what else we get from them.

### KAJA

What?

### KENDRA

Hamburgers.

### KENDRA and KAJA

Ha, ha, ha.

KENDRA and KAJA laugh and cross the stage, disappear again, and reappear instantly, continuing their tour.

### ZOO TOUR GUIDE

The next exhibit shows our rare South American tropical birds.

*Picture of a tropical bird appears, and the audience responds. Picture disappears.*

LEADER has children "caw" like tropical birds.

KENDRA and KAJA cover their heads as they cross the stage, disappear, and reappear, continuing their tour.

### KENDRA

Cover your head, Kaja!

### ZOO TOUR GUIDE

And now for our monkey exhibit.

SKIT SEVEN: GOD RULES!

*Picture of a monkey appears, and the audience responds. Picture disappears.*

KAJA and KENDRA stare open-mouthed.

*Picture of monkey reappears, and the audience responds. Picture disappears.*

KENDRA stares at the audience as if intrigued by the monkeys.

KAJA moves to follow the tour and then notices that KENDRA isn't following.

KAJA returns to KENDRA.

KENDRA points to audience.

KAJA tugs at KENDRA, but KENDRA won't budge.

KENDRA moves to the other side of the stage.

KENDRA looks at KAJA and then looks around, bending a bit lower so kids can't see her hand. Have a puppeteer attach a wrapped piece of gum to her hand.

## ZOO TOUR GUIDE

Our zoo rules state that you cannot feed the monkeys. Monkeys can bite, so it's dangerous to feed them. Also, they need a special diet that the zoo supplies so they can stay healthy.

Let's move on to view the zebras.

## KAJA

Hey, are you coming? We can't lose the tour.

## KENDRA

Look at those monkeys. Aren't they cute?

## KAJA

Yeah, they are. Come on, let's catch up with the tour.

## KENDRA

I want to get a closer look at these monkeys. Do you have anything we can feed them?

## KAJA

(**Shocked**) No way! It's against the rules to feed the animals.

## KENDRA

Well, the monkeys look hungry. Come on, what do you have? Maybe I have something...

## KAJA

I don't have anything! And I'm not going to break the rules.

KENDRA holds up her hand with the gum attached.

KENDRA's hand moves to the side of the stage, out of the children's view, looking as though she has passed her gum to a monkey. A puppeteer removes the gum.

KENDRA and KAJA look more closely off to the side of the stage, where KENDRA handed off the gum.

KAJA and KENDRA take a step back each time KAJA says "bigger."

KENDRA and KAJA exit the stage.

*While the ZOO TOUR GUIDE talks, puppeteers attach a rag to KENDRA's hand and another rag to KAJA's hand. Have a puppeteer hold a bucket in place for the characters to clean with.*

 **Stop the CD.**

## SCENE 2: The Cleanup

 **Play track 14 on CD A.**

KAJA and KENDRA appear, carrying their cleaning supplies.

## KENDRA
Hey, I've got a piece of gum right here. Maybe I can get the little monkey to come closer.

Look, he's coming closer. He's putting the gum into his mouth and chewing it. What's he doing now? He's...

## KAJA
Blowing a bubble! I didn't know monkeys could do that. It's getting bigger...and bigger... and bigger...

## KAJA and KENDRA
Ewww...Groooooosss...

## ZOO TOUR GUIDE
The zoo's rules must be obeyed. Since you've chosen to break the "No feeding the monkeys" rule, our very clever monkey has blown the world's largest bubble, which has burst all over the cage bars. Hmmm...What will be your punishment?

## KAJA
**(Sadly)** Now we have to clean up the monkey cage, all because you chose to break the rules.

KENDRA looks around.

**KENDRA**

I can see why the zoo wants people to obey the rules. I made a bad choice. Boy, that was some messy bubble.

**KAJA**

Well, let's start cleaning and get this over with.

**KENDRA**

Yeah. I'll make a better choice next time. Rules are meant to be followed.

KAJA and KENDRA act like they're wiping gum off the cage. They respond as they exit.

**KAJA and KENDRA**

Ewwww... Grooooooosss...

**THE END!**

# Who's Number One?

**Topic:** Heroes
**Scriptures You Might Read:** Exodus 20:2-3; 1 Kings 18:16-40

**Scene 1:** Outside a mall
**Scene 2:** Inside a stationery store
**Scene 3:** Outside a mall

## Characters
**MARISA:** a young girl who wants to buy a prayer journal
**STEVE:** a young boy who wants to get an autograph
**LEADER:** interacts with the audience

**Props:** You'll need a paper bag.

**Setup:** None

---

**SCRIPT**

| ACTIONS | WORDS |
|---|---|
| LEADER enters, stands in front of the puppet stage, and welcomes the audience. | **LEADER**<br>Welcome, everyone! Today's skit is called "Who's Number One?" Before we watch it, I was wondering if anyone knows what a hero is. |
| Pause for children to respond. | A hero is someone you might put as number one in your life. You think that person is the neatest thing going. A hero might be an athlete, an actor, or even a family member. Who are some of your heroes? |
| Pause for children to respond. | We may have lots of heroes in our lives. It's not bad to have heroes, as long as we remember that God wants to be number one in our lives. God deserves to be number one because he is the one true God. During |

59

today's skit, every time you hear someone say, "God's number one," cheer as loud as you can. Stop cheering when you see me hold out my hands like this. Let's try it a few times.

*Motion with both hands out in a "stop" gesture. Practice a few times, then on with the show!*

## SCENE 1: Outside the Mall

 *Play track 15 on CD A.*

MARISA and STEVE enter from stage left.

### MARISA
It's fun to go shopping at the mall. We gotta hurry, though, 'cause my dad's picking us up at 3:30.

### STEVE
No problem.

MARISA and STEVE stop center stage and look at each other.

### MARISA
All we have to buy are two notebooks to use as prayer journals. It'll be neat to write down our prayers.

### STEVE
I don't know if we'll have time to shop for those.

MARISA tilts her head as if questioning STEVE.

### MARISA
What do you mean? That's why we came to the mall.

STEVE bounces up and down with excitement.

### STEVE
I know, but I heard that José DeMarco is signing autographs at Sport World today, and he's my hero!

STEVE makes some swings as MARISA swerves to stay out of his way.

### STEVE
I want to be just like José DeMarco. When I'm old enough, I'm gonna play baseball for

**60**

MARISA stares at STEVE.

the Explorers too. I'm going to be the world's greatest hitter.

**MARISA**

I thought you wanted to buy a prayer journal.

**STEVE**

Sure, as long as I have enough time after I get my autograph from José DeMarco. He's my hero.

**MARISA**

Come on, let's get our prayer journals first. Talking with God is more important than talking with José DeMarco.

**STEVE**

I don't know about that...José DeMarco has hit a lot of home runs.

**MARISA**

Everything in the world is not about baseball, Steve. God is number one. Now, let's go.

LEADER encourages audience to cheer and then stop on cue.

MARISA and STEVE exit stage right.

**STEVE**

OK, OK! Batter up!

 **Puppeteers change the background (if any) to the stationery store scene. Stop the CD.**

## SCENE 2: The Stationery Store

 **Play track 16 on CD A.**

MARISA and STEVE enter from stage right.

**MARISA**

The ad said the notebooks were on sale at this store—only four dollars each!

| | |
|---|---|
| STEVE's head is hanging, and he appears to be depressed. | **STEVE**<br>I can't believe it. |
| | **MARISA**<br>Yeah, that's a pretty good price. I'm going to buy a green one. |
| STEVE shakes his head slowly from side to side. | **STEVE**<br>It's just not right. |
| MARISA looks at STEVE. | **MARISA**<br>OK, then I'll buy a red one. |
| STEVE continues to shake his head. | **STEVE**<br>It's just not fair. |
| MARISA does a double take. | **MARISA**<br>All right then, you can buy the red one. I'll buy the yellow one. |
| STEVE looks up. | **STEVE**<br>I'm going to call them. |
| | **MARISA**<br>Why? Don't they have the color you want? |
| STEVE snaps out of his dazed stupor. | **STEVE**<br>What? |
| MARISA tilts her head as she looks at STEVE. | **MARISA**<br>Are we talking about the same thing? |
| | **STEVE**<br>José DeMarco wasn't at Sport World. How could he not be there? Doesn't he know that he's my hero? |
| | **MARISA**<br>I was talking about the notebooks that we can use as prayer journals. |

**62**

**STEVE**

I was talking about José DeMarco.

MARISA marches back and forth, building up steam.

**MARISA**

Of course you were! You're always talking about José DeMarco. Steve, I'm sorry he wasn't at Sport World, but talking to José is not the most important thing in life. Why don't you concentrate on talking to God? God is number one.

LEADER encourages audience to cheer and then stop on cue.

STEVE stares out into space, hardly listening to MARISA.

**STEVE**

Talking to God? What do you mean?

STEVE continues to stare, oblivious to MARISA preaching to him.

**MARISA**

That's what prayer is. It's talking to God. These journals will help us remember our prayers. We can take notes when we read our Bibles, too, because God talks to us in his Word.

MARISA notices STEVE isn't paying much attention.

Ohhhh…

MARISA exits stage left, leaving STEVE staring into space.

I'm going to buy the green one.

**STEVE**

Right, the green one. Hmm…I wonder what color José DeMarco would choose…

***Puppeteers attach a paper bag to Marisa's hand backstage, while STEVE continues to stare into space and mumble on stage.***

MARISA re-enters from stage left, carrying a paper bag.

**MARISA**

We have to meet my dad soon.

| | |
|---|---|
| STEVE snaps out of it and looks at MARISA. | **STEVE**<br>I'll see you at the front of the mall. |
| | **MARISA**<br>You don't have your prayer journal yet. Are you going to buy one? |
| STEVE nods his head. | **STEVE**<br>Buy one? Yes, I am. |
| | **MARISA**<br>Which one are you going to buy? |
| STEVE starts out slowly and then gets energized thinking about finally finding José DeMarco. | **STEVE**<br>I'm going to…go buy one…*go by one* more store where José DeMarco might be. |
| STEVE jumps up and down, barely able to wait to go find his hero. | Maybe José was going to be at Toy World, not Sport World. I'll see ya out in front of the mall, Marisa. |
| STEVE darts off stage right, leaving a bewildered MARISA who calls after him. | **MARISA**<br>OK, but don't be late! |
| MARISA exits stage left. | |

 ***Puppeteers change the background (if any) to outside the mall. Stop the CD.***

## SCENE 3: Outside the Mall

 ***Play track 17 on CD A.***

| | |
|---|---|
| MARISA rushes in from stage left. | **MARISA**<br>I made it! But where's Steve? |
| MARISA looks up, down, all around. | Steve said he wanted to check out one more place to see if José DeMarco was there. He should be here any minute. |

| | |
|---|---|
| MARISA looks up, whistles a tune, and then yawns. | **MARISA**<br>Yawwwwwnnnn...<br><br>That Steve...He's letting his thoughts about José DeMarco crowd out any thoughts about God. I think Steve traded in his brain for a baseball. |
| STEVE rushes on from stage left. | **STEVE**<br>I'm here! I'm here! |
| MARISA looks at STEVE. | **MARISA**<br>Well, it's about time! Did you get your prayer journal? |
| STEVE looks out at the audience. | **STEVE**<br>What prayer journal? |
| | **MARISA**<br>The prayer journal we came to buy, silly. Did you get one to write in? |
| STEVE hangs his head down. | **STEVE**<br>No. I didn't get to that. I didn't even get José DeMarco's autograph. He wasn't at Toy World either. |
| | **MARISA**<br>Maybe you've got the wrong hero. |
| STEVE looks at MARISA. | **STEVE**<br>Are you kidding? José DeMarco wiped out six major league teams last year. You can't wipe out more than that. |
| MARISA nods her head. | **MARISA**<br>Oh, yes, you can! Jesus wiped out sin and death on the cross. That's pretty awesome if you ask me. Faith in José DeMarco does not forgive your sins or give you eternal life. |

STEVE looks out at the audience.

**STEVE**
Hmmm...I think I should've spent more time on the right hero.

MARISA holds up the paper bag.

**MARISA**
Cheer up. I thought you might run out of time, so I bought an extra journal for you.

**STEVE**
Wow, Marisa! Now you're my hero!

**MARISA**
Very funny, Steve! Who's number one in your life?

**STEVE**
God's number one. He's our *real* hero!

LEADER encourages audience to cheer and then stop on cue.

STEVE and MARISA exit stage right.

**STEVE and MARISA**
There's our ride!

**THE END!**

# What Would Jesus Watch?

**Topic:** Choices
**Scriptures You Might Read:** Ephesians 6:10-18; Philippians 4:8

**Scene:** A video store

**Characters**
MAUDE: a young girl in charge of her friends' choice of videos
TODD: young friend who's learning to make a good choice
ROD: another friend who's learning

**Props:** You'll need an empty video cover for each puppet and two poster-board signs on sticks: "Wow! Good choice!" and "Yuck! Bad choice!"

**Setup:** Give the video covers and signs to two puppeteers, and have them sit backstage.

Before the skit, practice reading the words on the signs with the audience.

---

### SCRIPT

| ACTIONS | WORDS |
|---|---|

 **Play track 18 on CD A.**

MAUDE, TODD, and ROD enter excitedly from stage right.

**MAUDE**

I'm so excited! We get to have a film festival and watch movies all day. Here's the deal, though. You each get to rent one video, but before you pick one, ask yourself, "What would Jesus watch?"

**ROD**

OK, I'll be back in a flash with my favorite video.

ROD quickly exits stage left. A puppeteer attaches a video to his hand.

TODD looks at MAUDE.

**TODD**

Why do we have to ask, "What would Jesus watch?"

| | |
|---|---|
| MAUDE motions with her hand as she talks. | **MAUDE**<br>Well, Jesus is always with us, right? So if we're watching a movie, we need to remember that Jesus is right there with us. And we all know that Jesus wants us to choose things that are good for us because he loves us! |
| | **TODD**<br>I never thought of it that way. I'll go pick a video now. See ya! |
| TODD quickly exits stage left. A puppeteer attaches a video to his hand. | |
| MAUDE walks to stage right and reaches out of view as if finding a video. A puppeteer attaches a video to her hand, and she walks back to her original position. | **MAUDE**<br>(Hums to herself.) |
| ROD races in from stage right with his video. | **ROD**<br>Yo, Maude! I've got my video. |
| MAUDE looks at ROD. | **MAUDE**<br>Hi, Rod. Whatcha' got? |
| ROD holds up his video. | **ROD**<br>This is the coolest video of all time. It's called *Haunted Hats*. |
| **"Yuck! Bad choice!" sign enters, and the audience responds. Sign exits.** | |
| MAUDE looks at the video. | **MAUDE**<br>What's it about? |
| ROD waves the video and then reads from the video jacket. | **ROD**<br>It's about these scary hats that try to land on people's heads. Listen to this, "You'll have nightmares for a whole year after watching this movie." |

| | |
|---|---|
| MAUDE shakes her head. | **MAUDE**<br>Rod, do you really think Jesus would watch that video? I'd rather get a good night's sleep. |
| | **ROD**<br>OK then, I'll be right back. |
| ROD quickly exits stage left. | |
| TODD quickly enters stage right. | **TODD**<br>I got it, Maude. Right here, the best video. |
| MAUDE looks at TODD. | **MAUDE**<br>Hi, Todd. What's it called? |
| TODD waves his video. | **TODD**<br>*Karate Karaoke.* |
| **"Yuck! Bad choice!" sign enters, and the audience responds. Sign exits.** | |
| MAUDE looks at the video. | **MAUDE**<br>What's it about? |
| TODD reads from the video jacket. | **TODD**<br>It's a group of Las Vegas singers who learn karate and fight in a no-rules tournament. The back says, "Nonstop kicking, punching, and singing." |
| MAUDE shakes her head. | **MAUDE**<br>Do you think that's a movie Jesus would watch? |
| TODD shakes his head and then exits stage left quickly. | **TODD**<br>Well...Come to think of it, I'm not so sure it's a movie I'd want to watch. OK, I'll be right back. |
| ROD quickly enters stage right. | **ROD**<br>This is it, Maude. I found the perfect video. |

SKIT NINE: WHAT WOULD JESUS WATCH?

| | |
|---|---|
| MAUDE looks at ROD. | **MAUDE**<br>Oh, good, Rod. What's it called? |
| ROD reads from the video cover. | **ROD**<br>*Wash Your Mouth Out.* |
| **"Yuck! Bad choice!" sign enters, and the audience responds. Sign exits.** | |
| MAUDE does a double take. | **MAUDE**<br>What is that about? |
| ROD excitedly walks back and forth. | **ROD**<br>I guess it's just about a bunch of kids who are really rude and say lots of bad words. The box says it's really funny. |
| | **MAUDE**<br>That doesn't sound very funny to me. |
| ROD quickly exits stage left. | **ROD**<br>I know, I know...Jesus probably wouldn't watch that video. OK, I'll be right back. |
| MAUDE works up steam and paces back and forth. Then ROD and TODD join MAUDE. | **MAUDE**<br>Guys, God says he really cares what we watch and think about. |
| ROD tilts his head to the right. | **ROD**<br>Really? |
| TODD tilts his head to the right also. | **TODD**<br>Where does God say that? |
| MAUDE continues pacing. | **MAUDE**<br>In Philippians 4:8, God tells us, "Finally, brothers, whatever is true, whatever is noble, whatever is right, whatever is pure, whatever is lovely, whatever is admirable—if anything is excellent or praiseworthy—think about such things." |

| | |
|---|---|
| TODD tilts his head to the left. | **TODD**<br>Really? |
| ROD tilts his head to the left too. | **ROD**<br>God said that? |
| MAUDE continues pacing. | **MAUDE**<br>Yes! God knows that we do the things we fill our minds with, so we have to be careful to fill our minds with good ideas and good things to do. |
| TODD puts his head straight and then exits quickly stage left. | **TODD**<br>Wow, I never thought about that before. I'll be right back. |
| ROD puts his head straight and then exits quickly stage left. | **ROD**<br>I've never thought about that either. I'll be right back. |
| TODD enters quickly stage right. | **TODD**<br>This is really it, Maude. |
| | **MAUDE**<br>OK, Todd, what is it? |
| TODD reads from the cover. | **TODD**<br>*Friends Forever.* It's the story of a cat and a bird. |
| **"Wow! Good choice!" sign enters, and the audience responds. Sign exits.** | |
| MAUDE nods. | **MAUDE**<br>Sounds great. |
| ROD re-enters quickly stage right. | **ROD**<br>I found it, Maude. This is a super video. I never even knew it existed. |
| | **MAUDE**<br>What is it, Rod? |

| | |
|---|---|
| ROD waves the video. | **ROD**<br>*Olympic Champions!* |
| *"Wow! Good choice!" sign enters, and the audience responds. Sign exits.* | |
| ROD jumps up and down. | **ROD**<br>Can you believe it? There's a video about all these cool athletes! I can't wait to watch it. |
| | **TODD**<br>What video did you get, Maude? |
| MAUDE holds up her video. | **MAUDE**<br>*Unforgettable Journeys.* It's the story of a hot air balloon trip around the world. |
| *"Wow! Good choice!" sign enters, and the audience responds. Sign exits.* | |
| TODD nods his head. | **TODD**<br>Sounds great. |
| ROD nods his head. | **ROD**<br>Yep. Definitely uplifting. |
| MAUDE nods her head. | **MAUDE**<br>For us and for God, too. |
| TODD jumps up and down. | **TODD**<br>Let's go! |
| ROD jumps up and down too. | **ROD**<br>The sooner we get back, the sooner we can watch these cool movies. |
| MAUDE joins them in jumping up and down. | **MAUDE**<br>It's going to be a great night at the movies! |
| MAUDE, TODD, and ROD exit quickly stage right. | |

**THE END!**

# A Good Horse

**Topic:** Obedience
**Scriptures You Might Read:** 1 Samuel 15:22; Matthew 3:13-17

**Scene:** High-Riding Dude Ranch

**Characters**
**DOUG:** a young boy who wants to take a risk on a horseback ride
**KYLIE:** a young girl who wants to be sure of a good ride
**RODEO BOB:** a man who helps them know the importance of listening to the One who leads you

**Props:** You'll need cowboy costumes (such as cowboy hats or bandannas).

**Setup:** Dress the puppets in cowboy costumes.

## SCRIPT

| ACTIONS | WORDS |
| --- | --- |
|  **Play track 19 on CD A.**<br><br>KYLIE and DOUG enter from stage right, and RODEO BOB enters from stage left.<br><br>KYLIE and DOUG nod their heads "yes." | **RODEO BOB**<br>Well, howdy there, Kylie and Doug! Welcome to High Ridin' Dude Ranch. Are you ready for the ride of your life?<br><br>Well, you've come to the right place. We've got all kinds of horses for you to choose from. We've got some great horses, and we've got some good ones. |
| DOUG and KYLIE do a double take at the same time. | **DOUG**<br>Did you say *great* horses and *good* horses? |
| | **RODEO BOB**<br>I sure did. |

RODEO BOB nods his head a couple of times for emphasis.

KYLIE shrugs.

**KYLIE**

What's the difference?

**RODEO BOB**

Well, missy, all of our horses are good, but some of our horses are great.

**KYLIE**

I don't get it. What do you mean?

**RODEO BOB**

Well, it's pretty simple, really. The great horses obey and "know who's boss" most all of the time. The good horses try, but don't always remember.

**DOUG**

You lost me.

**RODEO BOB**

Well, the great horses cost more money to rent because you'll always have a great time with them. These horses know who's leading them, and they obey.

**DOUG**

How much are the other horses...the good ones?

**RODEO BOB**

Well, the good ones are about half the price of the great ones because...well...they don't always obey the one who leads them. One guy rented one last week, and we're still looking for him. He and his horse never came back!

DOUG jumps excitedly up and down.

**DOUG**

I'm pretty good with horses, so I'll take the good horse!

| | |
|---|---|
| KYLIE shakes her head. | **KYLIE**<br>Not me! I want a great horse. |
| RODEO BOB points stage left, and DOUG and KYLIE exit that way. | **RODEO BOB**<br>OK, folks, head over thataway, and some guys will get ya set up. |
| RODEO BOB looks at the audience. | Y'all are about to learn a lesson on the importance of listening to the one who leads you! Ya gotta know who's boss. |
| Suddenly DOUG comes flying across from stage left to stage right as though he were riding on a wild horse. We don't see the horse, only DOUG bouncing madly. | **DOUG**<br>Ahhh! I said "whoa" not "go"! Ahhh! |
| RODEO BOB looks after DOUG and then out to audience. | **RODEO BOB**<br>See, that horse doesn't know who's boss. He's out of control. |
| KYLIE bounces gently on her "horse" as she crosses from stage left to stage right. She looks peacefully out to the audience. | **KYLIE**<br>I love my horse! She listens to everything I say. What a great ride! |
| RODEO BOB looks after KYLIE as she exits. | **RODEO BOB**<br>That's a great horse because she knows who's boss, and she obeys. |
| DOUG comes madly bouncing across from stage left to stage right, holding onto his hat. | **DOUG**<br>Heeeeelp! I wanna get off! |
| DOUG disappears. RODEO BOB looks out to the audience. | **RODEO BOB**<br>Well, folks, looks like some creatures have a hard time knowing who's boss. |
| | When you don't know who's boss, you don't know where you're goin' in life. It's an out-of-control, wild ride. |
| KYLIE comes clipping across the stage and peacefully moves over to RODEO BOB. | When you know who's boss and listen to who leads you, you stay on the right trail. |

**75**

We've got ourselves the best example in Jesus, ya see. Even though Jesus was and is God, he obeyed everything God the Father told him to do. Why, he even went down in the Jordan River and was baptized by John. One of the reasons he did that was because he wanted to show us how important it is to obey God. Jesus knows that when we disobey God, things don't go so well.

## DOUG
Whooooa!

## KYLIE
I'm going to do my best to follow Jesus' example. I'm going to obey and follow God.

## RODEO BOB
Good idea, Kylie. You're guaranteed to enjoy the ride.

**THE END!**

DOUG comes madly bouncing across from stage right to stage left, holding onto his hat.

# No Vacations

**Topic:** Prayer
**Scriptures You Might Read:**
Matthew 4:23-25; 11:28

**Scene:** The beach

**Characters**
SHERRY: a nine-year-old girl on the beach
PATTI: Sherry's friend
DAVE: Sherry's older brother

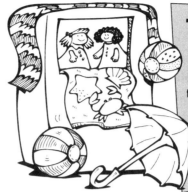

**Teacher Tip** Go all out with props and costumes for this beach scene. Attach bright-colored beach towels to the front of the puppet stage, use string or tape to attach inflated beach balls around the stage, and unfurl and prop up bright umbrellas.

**Props:** You'll need beachwear costumes (such as swim suits, robes, big hats); and puppet-size "beach towels"; and a sign on one side of the stage that says, "Warning: Stinging Jellyfish."

**Setup:** Dress the puppets in swimwear, or simply drape towels over their shoulders.

Before the skit, tell the audience that, every time they hear "What am I (are we) going to do?" during the skit, they'll shout "Take it to Jesus!" Practice a few times, then on with the show!

## SCRIPT

| ACTIONS | WORDS |
|---|---|
|  **Play track 1 on CD B.** | |
| All characters enter from stage right. DAVE moves slowly, head down. He's depressed. PATTI and SHERRY are happy and enter energetically. | **PATTI**<br>Hey, Dave, this is a good spot to grab. It's close to the water so we can swim all we want.<br><br>**DAVE**<br>(Sighs) Sure. |
| SHERRY puts an arm around DAVE. | **SHERRY**<br>Are you coming in with us, big brother of mine? |
| DAVE shakes his head "no." | **DAVE**<br>No, I think I'll just sit here and think about my friends at basketball practice. |

**77**

| | |
|---|---|
| SHERRY shakes DAVE. | **SHERRY**<br>Oh, forget about making the basketball team. You can't be good at everything. |
| | **DAVE**<br>Well, I'd like to be good at something. |
| | **SHERRY**<br>What about guitar? |
| | **DAVE**<br>Well, I suppose I'm OK... |
| | **SHERRY**<br>And fishing. You always catch fish. |
| DAVE lifts his head a little. | **DAVE**<br>Well, I did win last year's derby. |
| PATTI bounces up and down. | **PATTI**<br>And you're one of the nicest brothers I know. My brother would never take us to the beach. |
| DAVE lifts his head and then drops it back down, still depressed. | **DAVE**<br>Thanks, girls. I appreciate your trying to cheer me up, but it's no use. I just want to be alone for a while. I need a little vacation. |
| PATTI and SHERRY lean in together as they talk. | **PATTI**<br>Has he been like this all day? |
| | **SHERRY**<br>All week. |
| PATTI does a double take. | **PATTI**<br>You're kidding. He's really depressed, isn't he? |
| | **SHERRY**<br>I've never seen him so depressed. |

LEADER cues children to shout, "Take it to Jesus!"

**PATTI**
What are we going to do?

**SHERRY**
Let's pray for him.

**PATTI**
For him? Can't he pray for himself?

**SHERRY**
Sure he can, but Jesus wants us to pray for other people, too, not just for ourselves.

**PATTI**
OK.

PATTI and SHERRY bow their heads to pray.

**SHERRY**
Dear Jesus, please help Dave not to be so depressed. Help him to remember how much you love him. Then he won't be so sad about the basketball team.

PATTI and SHERRY nod their heads up and down as they say "Amen" together.

**PATTI and SHERRY**
Amen!

PATTI leans over so DAVE can hear her and shouts.

**PATTI**
OK, can we go swimming now?

DAVE nods his head.

**DAVE**
Sure.

(Sighs)

SHERRY and PATTI exit the side of the stage with the stinging jellyfish warning in the background. DAVE lies down, as if trying to soak up some sun, and rolls over once or twice, sighing.

| | |
|---|---|
| In a moment, PATTI races back in with SHERRY close behind. | **PATTI**<br>Ahh! I got stung by a jellyfish! It really hurts! |
| DAVE and SHERRY get on either side of PATTI to take care of her. DAVE leans out of the view of the audience and appears to spray PATTI. PATTI keeps wiggling around. | **DAVE**<br>Here, let me put some first-aid spray on it. |
| DAVE tilts his head back and yells. | Hold still! |
| PATTI tilts her head back and yells. | **PATTI**<br>My leg is swelling up. What are we going to do now? |
| LEADER cues children to shout, "Take it to Jesus!" | **SHERRY**<br>Let's pray. When we're hurt, tired, or sad, Jesus wants us to come to him. He loves us, and he'll help us. |
| All the CHARACTERS bow their heads. | Dear Jesus, please calm Patti down and let her leg feel better. |
| DAVE, SHERRY, and PATTI nod their heads at the same time as they say, "Amen!" | **DAVE, SHERRY, and PATTI**<br>Amen! |
| SHERRY helps PATTI move over to one side of the stage, and they sit down. | **SHERRY**<br>Let's sit and relax for a minute. I think the swelling will go down. |
| DAVE walks over to them. | **DAVE**<br>I'll go get the car, and we'll take you home. |
| DAVE exits stage right. | |
| PATTI hangs her head. | **PATTI**<br>Oh, no! Now our day at the beach is spoiled! |

| | |
|---|---|
| SHERRY pats PATTI's back. | **SHERRY**<br>It's OK. We can always come back another time. |
| DAVE comes racing back onto the stage. He almost runs over the girls. | **DAVE**<br>Somebody stole my car! |
| PATTI and SHERRY look at DAVE. | **PATTI and SHERRY**<br>What?! |
| DAVE tilts his head back and yells. | **DAVE**<br>My car is gone! Somebody took my car! |
| SHERRY stands. | **SHERRY**<br>Do something! Call the police! |
| DAVE nods his head and then exits stage right. | **DAVE**<br>Right. I'll call the police. |
| SHERRY helps PATTI stand. | **SHERRY**<br>What a day we're having! |
| PATTI shrugs. | **PATTI**<br>Well, what are we going to do now? |
| LEADER cues children to shout, "Take it to Jesus!" | Let me guess...Let's pray! |
| SHERRY nods. | **SHERRY**<br>You got it! |
| PATTI and SHERRY bow their heads. | Dear Jesus, this day just isn't turning out like we planned, but you want us to always come to you. Thanks for your promise that you're always with us. |
| PATTI and SHERRY nod their heads at the same time as they say, "Amen!" | **PATTI and SHERRY**<br>Amen! |

| | |
|---|---|
| DAVE re-enters the scene, slightly calmer now. | **DAVE**<br>I called the police. They said they would be here soon and give us a ride home. |
| PATTI hangs her head. | **PATTI**<br>I'm sorry this day was ruined. |
| DAVE pats PATTI's back. | **DAVE**<br>It wasn't ruined. All this helped me figure out that I was depressed about some pretty silly stuff. When I called the police, I was put on hold. So while I was waiting, I prayed really hard and gave everything I was worried about to Jesus. I feel better now. I don't know how everything will turn out, but I do know that God has a plan for our lives and he's with us forever. Jesus will take care of us. He loves us! |
| PATTI shakes her head. | **PATTI**<br>This is the prayingest family I've ever seen. |
| DAVE tilts his head as he asks the question. | **DAVE**<br>What do you mean? |
| PATTI waves a hand for emphasis as she explains. | **PATTI**<br>Sherry's been praying all day. Every time something goes wrong, she's praying. What if everybody in the whole world bothered Jesus with everything that goes on in everybody's life? Jesus would never get a vacation! |
| SHERRY hugs PATTI. | **SHERRY**<br>Jesus doesn't take vacations! He wants everyone to call him all the time. He can handle it because he's God. |
| DAVE and SHERRY get on either side of PATTI and help her. They exit stage right. | **DAVE**<br>Come on, girls. We're being rescued. I told you Jesus would take care of us. |

PATTI pops her head back in view of the audience.

LEADER cues children to shout, "Take it to Jesus!"

PATTI exits after she says her line.

## PATTI
Wow! I think I learned a lesson. The next time I wonder "What am I going to do?"...

...I'll remember to take my problems or worries to Jesus and trust that he'll take care of me.

**THE END!**

# Sugar or Salt

**Topic:** Sharing Our Faith
**Scripture You Might Read:** Matthew 5:13-16

**Scene:** Morton's living room

**Characters**
**MORTON:** a young boy who thinks salt is best
**DOMINO:** a young girl who learns a lesson

**Teacher Tip** If you can't find a lightweight cookbook, make one by folding a sheet of construction paper in half. Use a black marker to write "Cookbook" on one side of it.

**Props:** You'll need Bibles, a flashlight, a lightweight cookbook, unsalted popcorn, salted popcorn, and several bowls.

**Setup:** Give the flashlight to the leader. Keep the cookbook and two small bowls of popcorn backstage. Fill several bowls with popcorn—some bowls with salted popcorn and some with unsalted popcorn. Place at least one Bible out in the audience.

## SCRIPT

| ACTIONS | WORDS |
|---|---|
| **Play track 2 on CD B.**<br><br>MORTON enters from stage left, and DOMINO follows along. | **DOMINO**<br>And, Morton, my mama says I'm sweet as sugar. Isn't that great? |
| | **MORTON**<br>I guess so, but I'd rather be salt. |
| DOMINO shakes her head. | **DOMINO**<br>Salt? No way! Salt isn't sweet! |
| | **MORTON**<br>Of course not. It's salty. |
| | **DOMINO**<br>But Morton, everyone loves sweet things, like strawberry ice cream with whipped cream on top. |

**Teacher Tip** Have puppeteers backstage hold up the bowls of popcorn for the puppets during the skit. Have them place their hands beneath each bowl, keeping the bowls level and low so the audience can't see their hands. Or use paper bags instead of bowls for the puppets' popcorn.

**84**

| | |
|---|---|
| MORTON rubs his tummy. | **MORTON**<br>Mmmm! Sounds good, but are you *sure* you wouldn't rather be salt? |
| DOMINO nods her head. | **DOMINO**<br>Sure, I'm sure. What about your favorite ooey gooey chocolate brownies? They have lots of sugar in them. |
| MORTON smacks his lips. | **MORTON**<br>You're making me hungry. I do like those, but I just can't imagine what the world would be like without salt. |
| DOMINO holds up both hands. | **DOMINO**<br>Morton! What is it with you and salt? |
| | **MORTON**<br>You know, Domino, I'm glad you asked. |
| | **DOMINO**<br>Really? Why is that? |
| | **MORTON**<br>Because I've been reading about salt in the Bible. |
| | **DOMINO**<br>Salt's in the Bible? Are you sure you weren't looking in a cookbook? |
| MORTON shakes his head "no." | **MORTON**<br>No, it wasn't in a cookbook. Jesus says in the Bible that we're supposed to be the salt of the earth and let our light shine for him. |
| DOMINO shakes her head. | **DOMINO**<br>Salt? Jesus wants us to be more like sugar than salt. Jesus wants us to be sweet to everyone. Look it up if you don't believe me. |

| | **MORTON** |
| --- | --- |
| | That's a good idea. Just a minute. |
| MORTON exits stage right. Crashing and clanging noises are heard. While MORTON is gone, DOMINO looks after him, scratches her head, and reacts to the clanging noises. | |
| | Hey, I can't see. Can someone shine a light for me? |
| LEADER shines a flashlight backstage as if helping MORTON see better. | |
| MORTON re-enters carrying a cookbook, and the LEADER turns off the flashlight. | Hey, thanks. That's much better. |
| DOMINO points to the book. | **DOMINO** |
| | Morton! That's a cookbook! |
| MORTON looks at the book. | **MORTON** |
| | **(Surprised)** It is? Oh, it is! Sorry, just a minute. |
| MORTON exits stage right. Crashing and clanging noises are heard. DOMINO looks after him and reacts to the noise. | |
| | Hey, I can't see. Can someone shine a light for me? |
| LEADER turns on the flashlight and shines it backstage. | Thanks! I needed the light. |
| MORTON returns empty handed. LEADER turns off the flashlight. | |
| | **DOMINO** |
| | So where is your Bible? |
| MORTON holds out one hand. | **MORTON** |
| | I think I left it at Sunday school. |
| DOMINO tips her head to one side. | **DOMINO** |
| | So how are we going to look it up and find out what Jesus really said? |

SKIT TWELVE: SUGAR OR SALT

MORTON looks out at the audience.

DOMINO looks at the audience and points.

MORTON and DOMINO wave.

**LEADER stops the CD,** helps a person find the verse, and then escorts the child to the puppet stage.

Child brings the Bible to MORTON and holds it up. MORTON leans over and prepares to read. **Play track 3 on CD B.**

LEADER has the child sit close to the puppet stage and keep his or her place in the Bible.

DOMINO looks at the Bible.

MORTON starts to exit, then talks to the LEADER. The LEADER shines the flashlight, and MORTON exits. Clanging sounds and then the sound of popcorn popping can be heard. DOMINO looks after MORTON, then looks at the child, then back to where MORTON disappeared.

MORTON re-enters carrying two bowls of popcorn. He holds one out to DOMINO.

## MORTON
I know...Maybe someone else around here has a Bible.

## DOMINO
Morton, there's someone with a Bible.

## MORTON
Hey, would you look up Matthew chapter 5, verse 13 for me and bring it up here so I can read it?

Thanks! Here it is: "You are the salt of the earth."

## DOMINO
Morton, it does say salt! Thanks for holding the Bible...But what does it mean that we "are the salt of the earth"?

## MORTON
Wait right here and I'll show you.

Here we go. Hey...I'll need that light too!

SKIT TWELVE: SUGAR OR SALT

DOMINO sniffs the bowl of popcorn.

 **Stop the CD.**

DOMINO eats from the first bowl. The LEADER passes around the bowls of unsalted popcorn to the audience and then asks how they like it.

 **Play track 4 on CD B.**

MORTON holds out the same bowl.

DOMINO shakes her head.

MORTON offers the second bowl.

DOMINO hesitates, so MORTON moves the bowl closer.

 **Stop the CD.**

DOMINO tastes the new popcorn. The LEADER passes the bowls of salted popcorn to the kids in the audience and then asks how they like it.

 **Play track 5 on CD B**

DOMINO tries some more popcorn.

DOMINO continues to eat.

**DOMINO**
Mmm, popcorn!

**MORTON**
Here, Domino. Want some more of this popcorn?

**DOMINO**
No, thanks. There's something wrong with that popcorn!

**MORTON**
Here, try this one.

Oh, just try it.

**MORTON**
Well, what do you think?

**DOMINO**
I think this is really great popcorn. I could eat the whole bowl.

88

| | |
|---|---|
| MORTON looks in the bowl. | **MORTON**<br>You *did* eat the whole bowl, Domino. |
| | **DOMINO**<br>What made the difference between the two types of popcorn? |
| MORTON holds out first bowl of popcorn. | **MORTON**<br>Well, one bowl of popcorn didn't have any salt on it, but the bowl that you couldn't get enough of did. |
| | **DOMINO**<br>Awesome! It was the salt that made me want more! |
| | **MORTON**<br>When you ate the unsalted popcorn, you didn't want any more. When you ate the salted popcorn, you ate the whole bowl. That's what Jesus meant when he said, "You are the salt of the earth." |
| | **DOMINO**<br>I get it. If we can be "salty" and give others a little taste of Jesus, we can help them want more and more of God. |
| MORTON puts an arm around DOMINO. | **MORTON**<br>Good thinking, friend! |
| MORTON looks at the leader. | **MORTON**<br>Can you hold up the Bible for us again? Jesus tells us something else in Matthew chapter 5, verse 16. |
|  **Stop the CD.** | |
| The LEADER helps the child hold up the Bible so MORTON can read it. **Play track 6 on CD B.** | Jesus also said, "Let your light shine before men, that they may see your good deeds and praise your Father in heaven." Thanks for holding the Bible for me. |

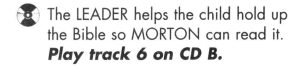

SKIT TWELVE: SUGAR OR SALT

LEADER has child sit down again.

## MORTON

Remember when the leader held the flash-light for me while I was looking around? The leader shined a light, and I could see! When we are *salt* and *light*, we help others see Jesus.

Let's go be salt and light and help others see Jesus.

DOMINO and MORTON exit together as DOMINO speaks to the leader.

## DOMINO

Cool! Will you shine the light for us again? We want to see where more of that salty popcorn is!

 **THE END!**

# Service With a Smile

**Topic**: Compassion
**Scriptures You Might Read:** Luke 10:25-37; Ephesians 4:32

**Scene 1:** Outdoors
**Scene 2:** Inside Mrs. Miller's house

## Characters
**ALYSSA:** a young girl with a servant's heart
**TOM:** her compassionate friend
**MRS. MILLER:** an elderly lady who receives help
**LEADER:** interacts with the audience

**Props:** You'll need a stick (to push so it looks like a vacuum), a rag, a bag for groceries, and the living room background (p. 9).

**Setup:** Mrs. Miller and her grocery bag need to be ready to enter soon after the skit begins.

······················· SCRIPT ·······················

| ACTIONS | WORDS |
|---------|-------|

### SCENE 1: Outdoors

 **Play track 7 on CD B.**

| | |
|---|---|
| ALYSSA and TOM enter from stage right and talk as they're walking. | **TOM**<br>That was nice of your sister to drop us off for ice cream. But why do we have to meet her at the church? |
| They stop center stage, looking at each other while they continue their conversation. | **ALYSSA**<br>She's working with her youth group on a new thing called "Service With a Smile." They do chores and nice things for people. |
| TOM shrugs. | **TOM**<br>Why? |

| | |
|---|---|
| ALYSSA puts her arm around TOM. | **ALYSSA**<br>Because God values compassion. Jesus was always helping people and caring for them. He even told stories, like the one about the good Samaritan who stopped and helped a man who was hurt. |
| TOM holds out a hand. | **TOM**<br>Why did Jesus care so much? |
| ALYSSA holds both arms up and looks up on "Jesus loves all of us." Then she walks a few steps in one direction and back toward TOM. | **ALYSSA**<br>Jesus loves all of us. And helping people is one of the best ways to show them that Jesus loves them. Then you can tell them about Jesus, who cares about them, too. |
| While TOM is talking, MRS. MILLER enters from stage right carrying a bag of groceries. She should be close to TOM when he says, "great big bowl." TOM spreads his arms wide and accidentally knocks over MRS. MILLER and her groceries. | **TOM**<br>Wow! That's pretty cool. Hey, speaking of cool…I can't wait to get ice cream! I'm gonna order a *great big bowl!* |
| MRS. MILLER raises an arm. | **MRS. MILLER**<br>Ouch! Help! Oh! |
| ALYSSA and TOM rush to either side of MRS. MILLER and lean down toward her. | **TOM**<br>Are you OK, ma'am? I'm sorry! I wasn't watching what I was doing. |
| | **MRS. MILLER**<br>Can you help me up? |
| TOM and ALYSSA bend over to help her up. | **TOM**<br>Sure. But be careful. Did you break anything? |
| | **MRS. MILLER**<br>Just my jar of pickles. |
| ALYSSA shakes her head. | **ALYSSA**<br>Oh, my goodness. This is just awful! |

SKIT THIRTEEN: SERVICE WITH A SMILE

**Stop the CD.** Puppeteers can have puppets freeze in position or disappear during the discussion so they can rest their arms.

LEADER steps in front of the puppet stage for a brief discussion with the audience.

Get several responses from the kids.

 **Play track 8 on CD B.** Puppets appear in previous positions.

TOM paces back and forth a bit.

MRS. MILLER motions with her hand.

TOM points to himself and then to ALYSSA.

MRS. MILLER gives a little bow.

ALYSSA and TOM bend down, out of the sight of the children, and then pop back up, as though they were picking up groceries. A puppeteer can be supporting the grocery bag from backstage.

MRS. MILLER nods her head.

## LEADER
What do you think Tom and Alyssa should do now? How could they care for Mrs. Miller?

Let's see how close your ideas are to the ideas Alyssa and Tom come up with.

## TOM
I can't believe I did that! I'm so sorry. What can I do for you?

## MRS. MILLER
Oh, I'll be all right, sonny.

## TOM
My name's Tom, and this is Alyssa.

## MRS. MILLER
My name is Mrs. Miller. So nice to meet you.

## ALYSSA
Here, let me help you. We can pick up your groceries.

## MRS. MILLER
That's mighty nice of you, Tom and Alyssa.

| | |
|---|---|
| TOM motions to the bag. | **TOM**<br>There, your groceries are all back in the bag. |
| | **ALYSSA**<br>Are you feeling all right, ma'am? You got knocked over pretty good! |
| MRS. MILLER starts to nod her head vigorously and then stiffens and places her hand on her back. | **MRS. MILLER**<br>Yes, I'll be all ri...Ouch! Oh, my back. |
| 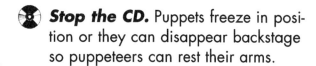 **Stop the CD.** Puppets freeze in position or they can disappear backstage so puppeteers can rest their arms. | |
| LEADER steps in front of the puppet stage and conducts a brief discussion. | **LEADER**<br>What do you think Tom and Alyssa should do now? How should they care for Mrs. Miller? |
| Get several responses. | |
|  **Play track 9 on CD B.** Puppets appear in their last positions. | Let's see how close your ideas are to the ideas Alyssa and Tom come up with. |
| TOM nods at ALYSSA and then at MRS. MILLER. | **TOM**<br>Hey, what if we walk you home, Mrs. Miller? Alyssa can carry the groceries, and I'll help you. |
| | **MRS. MILLER**<br>Well, that's very nice of you...if it's not too much trouble. |
| TOM appears to hand ALYSSA the groceries. | **TOM**<br>Of course it's not too much trouble. I knocked you over. This whole thing isn't your fault. Come on, I'll help you walk home. Here, Alyssa. |

## MRS. MILLER

Thank you. You're nice children.

TOM, ALYSSA, and MRS. MILLER exit stage left.

 **Puppeteers make a quick scene change to MRS. MILLER's living room. Stop the CD.**

## SCENE 2: Inside Mrs. Miller's House

 **Play track 10 on CD B.**

All characters enter stage left.

MRS. MILLER motions to her counter, then to her couch, and then hangs her head in frustration.

## MRS. MILLER

Here we are. I'm home now. Thank you very much. We can put the groceries over... Well, I don't really think I can lift the groceries from there. How about over here on the couch... Well, maybe not the couch. I really need to clean that up. How about... Well, I don't know where to put the groceries. I have so much housework to do, but I can't because my back has been bothering me so much.

 **Stop the CD.** Puppets freeze in position or disappear.

LEADER steps in front of the puppet stage and conducts a brief discussion.

## LEADER

What do you think Tom and Alyssa should do now? How could they care for Mrs. Miller?

Get several responses.

 **Play track 11 on CD B.** Puppets resume where they left off.

Mrs. Miller's back hurts so much that she can't clean up her own house. Let's see how close your ideas are to the ideas Alyssa and Tom come up with.

| | |
|---|---|
| ALYSSA pops up and then puts her arm around TOM. | **ALYSSA**<br>I have an idea! We'll clean up your house and put away your groceries for you. |
| MRS. MILLER shakes head from side to side in wonder. | **MRS. MILLER**<br>You will? Oh, my goodness! That's the nicest thing anybody has ever done for me. |
| ALYSSA gives TOM a little nudge | **ALYSSA**<br>Oh, that's OK. Tom loves to do dishes. |
| TOM nudges ALYSSA back. | **TOM**<br>I do? Right, I do, and Alyssa loves to vacuum. |
| ALYSSA and TOM bend down a bit out of view as if beginning to clean. Puppeteers attach a stick to ALYSSA for a vacuum and a rag to TOM. | **ALYSSA**<br>I do? Yes, he's right. I love to vacuum. Come on, let's get to work. |
| ALYSSA and TOM walk back and forth across the stage as though they're cleaning up the house. MRS. MILLER stands center stage looking in both directions as ALYSSA and TOM cross in front of her. | **MRS. MILLER**<br>Isn't this wonderful? I've never had this happen to me before. You're such lovely children. Why are you doing this for me? You don't even know me. |
| TOM talks as he continues to clean. | **TOM**<br>Well, we know you now. I can tell everybody I "bumped into" a new friend. |
| ALYSSA talks as she continues to clean. | **ALYSSA**<br>Very funny, Tom. We're almost finished! |
| TOM stops what he's doing. | **TOM**<br>Oh, no! We're late to meet your sister at the church. |
| MRS. MILLER walks over to TOM and ALYSSA | **MRS. MILLER**<br>The church? Oh, I understand now. You're Christian children. Do you go to that church up the street? |

| | **ALYSSA** |
|---|---|
| ALYSSA nods her head. | Yes, we do! Do you want to come with us this weekend? We could come and get you. Tom has to drop off a new jar of pickles for you anyway. Don't you, Tom? |
| | **TOM** |
| TOM does a double take and then nods his head. | (Surprised) Pickles, yeah, sure, pickles. I'll bring you a jar of pickles on the way to church. |
| | **MRS. MILLER** |
| | I've always wanted to go visit that church, but I was afraid to go by myself. Now I have someone to go with me. |
| | **ALYSSA** |
| ALYSSA puts an arm around MRS. MILLER. | That's it, then. We'll pick you up at 10:00 on Sunday. |
| | **MRS. MILLER** |
| | Thank you so much for helping me. |
| | **TOM** |
| TOM says to ALYSSA. | Come on, before your sister leaves and we don't get ice cream. |
| | **MRS. MILLER** |
| MRS. MILLER disappears, leaving TOM and ALYSSA looking in her direction. They bend down as if finishing their cleaning. Puppeteers remove the stick and rag. | Ice cream? Wait. I'll be right back. |
| MRS. MILLER enters and appears to hand ALYSSA and TOM some coins. | Here you go, dearies. Let me pay for your ice cream, as a way to say thank you for all the kindness and care you've shown me today. |
| | **ALYSSA** |
| ALYSSA shakes her head. | That's OK. My sister is going to pay for it. |

**97**

TOM jumps up and down.

MRS. MILLER waves.

ALYSSA and TOM wave as they exit stage left.

## MRS. MILLER
Well, take this money anyway, and eat twice as much ice cream!

## TOM
Twice as much ice cream! Awesome!

## MRS. MILLER
Go on now. You've given up so much of your day already. I'll see you on Sunday, and I'll be ready!

## ALYSSA and TOM
'Bye! God bless you!

## MRS. MILLER
He already has.

**THE END!**

# Amazing Surprise!

**Topic:** Jesus Is Risen
**Scriptures You Might Read:** Matthew 27:27-56; 28:1-10; Galatians 2:20

**Scene:** County Fair

**Teacher Tip** At the end of the skit, you could give each child a flower bulb to plant at home. When kids see the beautiful flowers grow, they'll be reminded that Jesus is risen from the dead. He's alive!

## Characters

**MOLLIE:** a girl who has never been to a county fair before
**MATTHEW:** a boy who wants to have a contest
**MCKENZIE:** a girl who thinks she's won first place
**LEADER:** interacts with the audience

**Props:** You'll need a paper sack, a flower bulb, and a bright flower in a pot.

**Setup:** Give the paper sack, flower bulb, and potted flower to a puppeteer, and have him or her sit backstage.

---

### SCRIPT

| ACTIONS | WORDS |
|---|---|
|  ***Play track 12 on CD B.***<br><br>MCKENZIE, MATTHEW, and MOLLIE enter from stage right. They talk as they walk. | **MOLLIE**<br>Oh, Matthew and McKenzie, I'm so excited to come to the county fair! I've never been to one before. Have you?<br><br>**MATTHEW**<br>I have, Mollie. It's so neat because sometimes the biggest animals you've ever seen are at a county fair. Their owners put them in fancy cages and corrals, and then the judges come by and pick the winner. |
| All characters stop center stage and continue to talk.<br><br>MCKENZIE looks at audience. | **MCKENZIE**<br>I went to a county fair a couple of years ago. There are crafts and yummy pies and cakes and jams! I guess a county fair is a place |

SKIT FOURTEEN: AMAZING SURPRISE!

**🔘 Stop the CD.** LEADER counts the number of kids who've been to a county fair.

**🔘 Play track 13 on CD B.**

where you'll find the most beautiful, most incredible, and biggest things you can imagine. How many of you have been to a county fair?

## MOLLIE, MCKENZIE, and MATTHEW

Cool!

## MATTHEW

Hey, I have an idea! Let's have a contest. Let's search these county fairgrounds and meet back here with a report of what we think is *the most* amazing thing we've ever seen. Then we'll vote on the winner! OK?

MATTHEW excitedly bounces up and down as he describes the contest idea.

MCKENZIE and MOLLIE nod at the same time.

## MCKENZIE and MOLLIE

OK! Great idea!

***Characters dart off stage left, one at a time. Puppeteers attach a paper bag to MCKENZIE's hand.***

MCKENZIE quickly enters stage right, carrying a plain paper bag.

## MCKENZIE

Am I first? I'm quick!

MCKENZIE talks to audience. Holds up paper bag.

You may think this is a plain old paper bag, but inside is the most amazing surprise. I know I'll win the contest! I'll show you what's in it later.

MATTHEW comes racing in stage right.

## MATTHEW

I found it! I saw the most amazing thing at the fair.

MOLLIE comes racing in stage right immediately after him.

## MOLLIE

Wait, you guys! I've seen the most amazing thing!

| | |
|---|---|
| MATTHEW points to himself. | **MATTHEW**<br>I saw a calf with two heads! Can you believe that? |
| MOLLIE opens her mouth in amazement and then points to herself. | **MOLLIE**<br>Wow! That's amazing! Well, I found a 25-pound carrot. |
| MATTHEW opens his mouth in amazement and then nods at MCKENZIE. | **MATTHEW**<br>Wow! That's amazing! What do you have, McKenzie? |
| MCKENZIE holds up the bag. | **MCKENZIE**<br>My amazing surprise is in this bag. |
| | **MOLLIE**<br>What is it? |
| | **MCKENZIE**<br>I'll tell you if you guys aren't going to change your minds about your most amazing thing. |
| MATTHEW tilts head as he asks the question. | **MATTHEW**<br>Why would we change our minds? |
| MCKENZIE hugs the bag. | **MCKENZIE**<br>Because if you're going to stick with what you've got, then you're going to lose the contest, because mine is much more amazing than a big carrot or a two-headed calf. |
| MATTHEW shakes his head. | **MATTHEW**<br>It doesn't look very amazing. |
| | **MOLLIE**<br>Yeah. What's so great about a brown paper sack? |
| | **MCKENZIE**<br>It's what's inside the sack that's so amazing. |

**MATTHEW**

OK, now I'm not so sure about my two-headed calf. I'll be right back. I saw something else.

MATTHEW quickly exits stage left.

**MOLLIE**

You've got me wondering too. Maybe my carrot isn't that big a deal. I'll be right back.

MOLLIE quickly exits stage left.

Speaks to audience.

**MCKENZIE**

I have no doubt that what's inside this bag is the most amazing thing!

MOLLIE comes racing in stage right.

**MOLLIE**

I win! I win!

MATTHEW comes racing in stage right.

**MATTHEW**

I win! I win!

**MOLLIE**

I found a roller-skating bear! Can you believe that?

MATTHEW acts like he's boxing.

**MATTHEW**

That's pretty amazing, but I can top that. I found a kangaroo boxing-match. They wear boxing gloves and everything. It's the most amazing thing I've ever seen!

MOLLIE and MATTHEW look at the bag.

**MOLLIE**

We haven't heard from McKenzie yet. She's just standing here with her little brown bag, and she looks pretty confident to me. So what's in the bag, McKenzie?

**MCKENZIE**

Are you really ready for me to tell you what's in my bag? You don't want to change your minds?

They shake their heads "no."

**MOLLIE and MATTHEW**

No!

MCKENZIE appears to be reaching inside her bag. A puppeteer holds up a large dried-up flower bulb—being sure to keep his or her hand out of view from the audience.

**MCKENZIE**

OK, here goes.

**MOLLIE**

What's that? Is it a rock?

MATTHEW takes a close look.

**MATTHEW**

Ooh...I think it's a dirt clod.

**MCKENZIE**

It's a flower bulb.

MOLLIE tilts her head as she asks the question.

**MOLLIE**

Umm...Why is that the most amazing thing you've ever seen?

MATTHEW nods.

**MATTHEW**

Yeah, I've seen lots of flower bulbs, but I've never seen a boxing kangaroo.

**MOLLIE**

Or a roller-skating bear.

MCKENZIE moves the bulb from MATTHEW to MOLLIE and back.

**MCKENZIE**

Well, I think this bulb is the most amazing surprise because it looks dead—all dried up and ugly. If you saw this bulb lying around, you'd probably throw it away, right?

Both nod.

**MATTHEW and MOLLIE**

Right.

## MCKENZIE

That's what's so amazing! Even though it looks completely dead, there's life and beauty inside of it. All you have to do is plant the bulb in the ground and a miracle happens. Out of this dead-looking bulb comes one of the most beautiful living things you've ever seen.

MCKENZIE reaches out of sight and appears to "drag" in a pot with a large, beautiful flower blooming in it. A puppeteer moves the pot from backstage.

## MOLLIE

Wow! That beautiful flower grew out of a dead-looking thing like this?

## MCKENZIE

That's right! I think it's pretty amazing that life could come from what appears to be dead. So who wins? Which one of us has seen the most amazing surprise?

All characters huddle with their heads bowed, as if deciding among themselves who will win.

 **Stop the CD.** Puppets either freeze or disappear during the discussion.

LEADER asks kids a couple of questions.

Get several responses.

## LEADER

Of all the things Matthew, McKenzie, and Mollie have seen at the county fair, which one do you think is the most amazing surprise? Why?

 **Play track 14 on CD B.** Puppets resume action.

## LEADER

Let's see which item they choose as the number-one, most amazing surprise.

MCKENZIE, MOLLIE, and MATTHEW look up, then huddle again with heads bowed.

| | |
|---|---|
| All characters put their heads up. | **MCKENZIE, MOLLIE, and MATTHEW**<br>The winner is...the bulb! |
| MCKENZIE holds up the bulb. | |
| MATTHEW motions to the bulb and then the flower. | **MATTHEW**<br>That's so amazing that a dead-looking thing like that bulb can make a beautiful, living thing like that flower. |
| | **MCKENZIE**<br>I'm going to buy this flower and the bulb. I want to take them home and plant the bulb. I really love this flower. |
| MATTHEW looks more closely at the flower. | **MATTHEW**<br>How can you love a flower? Do you have a name for it, too? |
| | **MCKENZIE**<br>Yes, I do. I'm going to call it Easter. |
| MOLLIE looks more closely at the flower. | **MOLLIE**<br>Easter? Don't you mean Esther? That's a girl's name. |
| | **MATTHEW**<br>How do you know it's a girl flower? Maybe it's a guy flower, and you should call it Ralph. |
| MCKENZIE nods toward the flower. | **MCKENZIE**<br>I'm naming it Easter because the bulb and flower remind me of Easter—the time when Jesus came alive again after he died for our sins. |
| MOLLIE puts her arms around MCKENZIE and MATTHEW. | **MOLLIE**<br>Because of Jesus, we'll live forever too. |

SKIT FOURTEEN: AMAZING SURPRISE!

All characters nod at the same time and then exit stage left. They appear to be taking the bulb and flower with them.

LEADER reads Galatians 2:20, prays, and then gives each child a flower bulb to plant as a reminder that Jesus died for us and is alive forever.

**MATTHEW**
Now *that's* amazing!

**THE END!**

# A Forever Hero

**Topic:** Sharing Our Faith
**Scriptures You Might Read:** Acts 6:8–7:60; 1 Peter 3:15

**Scene:** Kate's living room

## Characters
**KATE:** a young girl who's about to go to a Christian concert
**TASHI:** Kate's girlfriend who'll go with her
**DAVIS:** a friend who's sad about his favorite actor gone bad
**LEADER:** interacts with the audience

**Props:** You'll need the living room background (p. 9) and a poster-board sign on a stick that says, "Tell him about Jesus!"

**Setup:** Give the sign to a puppeteer, and have him or her sit backstage.

Before the skit, practice having the audience respond to the sign when it appears.

### SCRIPT

| ACTIONS | WORDS |
| --- | --- |

 **Play track 15 on CD B.**

| ACTIONS | WORDS |
| --- | --- |
| TASHI and KATE come bounding into the scene from stage right. Both are so happy that they can hardly contain themselves. | **KATE**<br>I can't believe we're going to an "I Believe" concert. They're my very, very favorite Christian band. Have you heard their new song called, "Hope, Don't Mope"? |
| TASHI and KATE keep talking and walking until they are center stage. | **TASHI**<br>No, but I can guess what it's about. It's about "hoping" to be with Jesus in heaven someday, so that you don't "mope" around and let your problems get to you. |
| | **KATE**<br>Exactly right! |
| DAVIS enters from stage left. He's very angry. | **DAVIS**<br>I can't believe it! It didn't happen! It couldn't happen! |

107

| | |
|---|---|
| KATE tilts her head to the left. | **KATE**<br>What didn't happen? |
| TASHI tilts her head to the left. | **TASHI**<br>What couldn't happen? |
| | **DAVIS**<br>It's terrible! |
| TASHI and KATE straighten up at the same time as they ask the question. | **TASHI and KATE**<br>What's so terrible? |
| DAVIS leans in closer and closer to the girls each time he says a phrase. | **DAVIS**<br>My all time favorite...the world famous actor...Sean Vincent...*robbed a gas station*! |
| Both girls move their heads up and down at the same time when they say their line. | **KATE and TASHI**<br>What?! |
| KATE and TASHI get on either side of DAVIS to comfort him. | **KATE**<br>What made him do that? |
| | **DAVIS**<br>He wasn't getting as many starring roles, and he was running out of money. |
| | **TASHI**<br>Still, that's no reason to rob a gas station! |
| DAVIS hangs his head. | **DAVIS**<br>I read that he has been really depressed. Acting was his life. |
| | **KATE**<br>Now he's a thief. |
| DAVIS is really animated as he talks. He twists from side to side, looking at both girls. | **DAVIS**<br>Yeah, can you believe it? I wanted to be just like him. I wanted to be in all kinds of action movies. Now I don't know what I want to do |

when I grow up. Who am I going to be like? What will I wear? How will I talk? What will I care about?

*"Tell him about Jesus!" sign appears, and the audience responds. Sign exits.*

TASHI and KATE point out to the audience as they say their line together.

## TASHI and KATE
Good idea!

 **Stop the CD.** Puppets freeze or disappear backstage.

LEADER has a brief discussion with kids. Pause after each question, and get several responses.

## LEADER
If you were Tashi and Kate, what would you tell Davis? What would you say about Jesus?

Let's see how Tashi and Kate help Davis learn about Jesus.

 **Play track 16 on CD B.** Puppets resume their action.

## TASHI
I know what you need.

DAVIS looks at TASHI.

## KATE
You need somebody who'll never let you down.

DAVIS looks at KATE.

## TASHI
Or rob a gas station.

DAVIS looks at TASHI.

## DAVIS
Who?

DAVIS looks out at the audience.

*"Tell him about Jesus!" sign appears, and the audience responds. Sign exits.*

TASHI and KATE point to the audience as they say their line together.

## TASHI and KATE
Good idea!

DAVIS continues to look back and forth between TASHI and KATE.

## TASHI
You need somebody who's so awesome that you'll want to be just like him.

**KATE**

Yeah, somebody that you'll be so impressed with that you'll want to say the kinds of things he wants you to say.

DAVIS looks out at the audience.

**DAVIS**

He sounds great! Is he famous?

DAVIS continues to look back and forth from KATE to TASHI.

**KATE**

You bet he is. He's the most famous person ever. There's even a book that tells about his exciting adventures.

**DAVIS**

OK! Who is it?

**TASHI and KATE**

Jesus!

DAVIS looks out at the audience.

**DAVIS**

Jesus?

DAVIS continues to look back and forth between TASHI and KATE.

**TASHI**

Jesus loves you and will never let you down. Jesus is with you everywhere you go, even when you're asleep!

**KATE**

Do you want to hear the whole story about Jesus tonight?

**DAVIS**

Tonight? What's going on tonight?

**KATE**

My dad gave me tickets to see my favorite Christian band, "I Believe," and I'm going to take you and Tashi.

DAVIS shrugs.

**DAVIS**

I believe in what?

KATE throws her arms wide.

**KATE**

I believe in Jesus. They sing about telling the whole world about Jesus' love.

TASHI throws her arms wide.

**TASHI**

They sing about Jesus' life and death and how he rose again. Because of Jesus, we'll live forever!

KATE and TASHI jump up and down.

**KATE**

Jesus is a "forever hero," not like Sean Vincent!

DAVIS nudges the two girls to exit stage right.

**DAVIS**

Let's go!

**THE END!**

# Worth Waiting For

**Topic:** Hope
**Scriptures You Might Read:** Acts 27; Romans 5:3-4; Hebrews 10:23

**Scene 1:** Family Room
**Scene 2:** Airport

## Characters

**ANNA:** a girl who has a sad problem
**MARITZA:** a helpful friend
**LEADER:** interacts with the audience

**Props:** You'll need party snacks, such as cheese, crackers, cookies, milk, and juice.

**Setup:** In a separate room, set up the snacks for a surprise party.

## SCRIPT

| ACTIONS | WORDS |
|---|---|

### SCENE 1: Maritza's Home

 **Play track 17 on CD B.**

| ACTIONS | WORDS |
|---|---|
| ANNA enters from stage right and walks slowly to center stage. She's depressed and stares out into the audience. MARITZA enters from stage left and joins her. | **MARITZA**<br>Here you are, Anna. I was wondering where you went. One minute you were watching TV with me, and the next minute you were gone. Are you OK? |
| | **ANNA**<br>(**Sighs**) Yeah, I'll be OK, I guess. |
| MARITZA gets closer to ANNA. | **MARITZA**<br>What's the matter? |
| | **ANNA**<br>It's my parents. They aren't getting along. |
| MARITZA puts her arm around ANNA. | **MARITZA**<br>Oh, Anna, I'm so sorry! |

## ANNA

I wish everyone wouldn't be so sad.

## MARITZA

When we go through tough times—or any time—God wants us to come to him. So let's say a prayer for you and your parents.

## LEADER

The Bible says that God is with us through the tough times. So we need to believe in Jesus and have hope! Think for a moment about yourself, a friend, or a family member who might be going through a tough time.

Does everyone have someone in mind? Let's pray for those people and ask God to be with them. Please fold your hands and bow your heads.

 **Stop the CD.** MARITZA and ANNA bow their heads.

LEADER reads Romans 5:3-4 and then leads a brief discussion with the kids.

Pause a moment.

LEADER prays in own words, offering the people and the situations to God and his loving care.

 **Play track 18 on CD B.**

Amen!
Let's see what happens with Maritza and Anna.

## MARITZA and ANNA

Amen!

MARITZA and ANNA look at each other.

## MARITZA

Besides praying, you know what else helps you get through hard times? Having something to look forward to. Then you don't think about the bad stuff so much.

## LEADER

Here's something for you to look forward to. At the end of the skit, you'll get a surprise. It'll be great—something worth waiting for!

 **Stop the CD again.**

LEADER talks to the kids.

**113**

**Play track 19 on CD B.**


ANNA stands straighter.


MARITZA puts her arms around ANNA
again.

**LEADER**
Let's see what Maritza's surprise is.

**ANNA**
I'd be up for something new!

**MARITZA**
Well, then get ready to feel better 'cause
we're going to do something special!

**ANNA**
Like what?

**MARITZA**
My big sister told me to pick some fun place
to go this weekend and she'd take me.
Instead of me picking the place, you pick it!

**ANNA**
Why me?

**MARITZA**
Because I'm your friend, and this is something I can do to help you take your mind
off your troubles. You need something to
look forward to, so you pick something, and
that's what we'll do.

ANNA tilts her head one way.

**ANNA**
Anything?

MARITZA nods.

**MARITZA**
Anything!

ANNA tilts her head the other way.

**ANNA**
Anywhere?

MARITZA nods.

**MARITZA**
Anywhere!

**114**

| | **ANNA**<br>I don't know what to do. |
| ANNA walks a few steps, stops, and looks down. | |
| | **MARITZA**<br>What have you always wanted to do, or where have you always wanted to go? |
| ANNA paces back and forth. | **ANNA**<br>Well, I uh...I think I'd like to...Well, you know what I really love? |
| | **MARITZA**<br>What? |
| | **ANNA**<br>Airplanes. |
| | **MARITZA**<br>Airplanes? Why airplanes? |
| ANNA continues pacing. MARITZA watches her go back and forth. | **ANNA**<br>I've never been in an airplane, but it seems to me like it would be the greatest thing in the world to fly up through the clouds and up, up, up, into the air. I just think it would be great. |
| | **MARITZA**<br>How about if I ask my sister to take us to the airport? Do you want to go there? |
| ANNA perks up. | **ANNA**<br>Really? We get to go see airplanes? |
| | **MARITZA**<br>Sure. |
| ANNA bounces up and down. | **ANNA**<br>Oh, I'd love to take a trip to the airport. Thank you! That's the nicest thing anybody's ever done for me. |

**MARITZA**

What are friends for if we can't cheer each other up? Besides, your problems don't look so big if you have something to look forward to, right?

**ANNA**

Right! It'll be a trip worth waiting for!

MARITZA and ANNA exit stage right.

**Puppeteers quickly change the background (if any) to an airport scene. Stop the CD.**

## SCENE 2: The Airport

 **Play track 20 on CD B.**

LEADER has kids in the audience spread their arms out like wings and make airplane noises.

ANNA and MARITZA enter from stage right. They stop center stage and look at the audience.

**ANNA**

Have you ever seen so many awesome airplanes?

**MARITZA**

There are so many of them!

LEADER motions for kids to stop.

ANNA looks up. MARITZA looks up, too.

**ANNA**

Someday, I'd like to be a pilot. I'd love to be able to fly above the clouds and see the world from way up there.

MARITZA looks at ANNA.

**MARITZA**

How are things with your parents?

ANNA looks at MARITZA.

**ANNA**

I think they're getting along a little better. I've been praying for them. I trust that

God's taking care of them, like he's taking care of me.

**MARITZA**

Hey, Anna, you know the feeling you get when you have something to look forward to—like coming on this trip to the airport?

Do you know what that feeling is called?

ANNA nods.

**ANNA**

No, I just know that, when I feel it, I'm not so sad anymore. I get happy because I'm thinking about something I love.

ANNA shakes her head.

**MARITZA**

That feeling is called "hope," and you're right. It means looking forward to something you love.

MARITZA walks a few steps in one direction.

We looked forward to coming to the airport, but this trip will end. Do you know a trip we can look forward to that will never end?

Then she walks back to ANNA.

**ANNA**

What? I'd really hope for something fun like that!

**MARITZA**

Someday we'll get to live forever with Jesus in heaven.

ANNA leans closer to MARITZA.

**ANNA**

Heaven will be awesome!

**MARITZA**

Yes, and believe me, it's a trip worth waiting for.

MARITZA and ANNA exit stage left.

LEADER leads kids to the room with the snacks. Enjoy the party. It was worth waiting for!

## THE END!

# Take a Bath

**Topic:** Unexpected Cure
**Scriptures You Might Read:** 2 Kings 5:1-16; 1 Peter 5:6

**Scene 1:** Elisha's front door
**Scene 2:** Naaman's home
**Scene 3:** The Jordan River

**Teacher Tip** You can use one puppet for both the Messenger and the Servant. Simply switch different-colored headpieces onto the puppet's head during a scene change.

## Characters

**NAAMAN:** a man who is looking for a cure for his leprosy
**MESSENGER:** a woman who works for the prophet Elisha
**SERVANT:** a person who works for Naaman

**Props:** You'll need seven adhesive bandages, Bible costumes, and eight poster-board signs on sticks: "Naaman, take a bath!" and "One," "Two," "Three," "Four," "Five," "Six," "Seven."

**Setup:** Dress the puppets in Bible costumes, and stick seven adhesive bandages on Naaman. Have at least two puppeteers sit backstage to hold the signs, make quick scene changes, and take the adhesive bandages off Naaman.

Before the skit, practice shouting the words on the signs with the audience.

## SCRIPT

| ACTIONS | WORDS |
| --- | --- |

### SCENE 1: Onward to Elisha's

 **Play track 21 on CD B.**

NAAMAN enters from stage left and stays stage left, walking in place and complaining.

**Teacher Tip**
Drape a blue sheet over the foreground for the Jordan River. Have two puppeteers backstage wave it up and down at the appropriate time during the skit.

**NAAMAN**

All these years I've had leprosy—a sickness that makes my skin very sore and not very nice to look at. I've tried everything under the sun for a cure. I tried rubbing a frog on my sores. That didn't work (but I did hop around and eat flies). I tried standing on my head and drinking a cup of water. That didn't work (but I didn't get the hiccups for a whole year). I even tried putting camel spit on myself every night before going to bed. That didn't work (but I didn't seem to get as thirsty).

Now, here I am trekking the desert because some simple servant girl tells my wife a rumor about a prophet. Supposedly, this prophet guy can cure leprosy. Ha!

**NAAMAN**

Naaman, Naaman, Naaman! You are a commander of a great army, and still you let that woman talk you into this. It probably means more trouble. Just like this morning when I stopped by to see the king. I wanted to get his permission to visit this Elisha prophet guy. And what happens? The king gets all upset.

NAAMAN shakes head while talking to himself as he continues walking in place.

He thinks I'm trying to pick a fight with him. **(Grumbles)** Oh, well, I'm almost there.

NAAMAN throws hands up in disgust. Continues grumbling as he arrives at Elisha's door, which is stage right.

NAAMAN knocks on door.

I sure hope this prophet Elisha isn't some kind of a quack.

**MESSENGER**

MESSENGER appears at the open door.

May I help you?

**NAAMAN**

May I see your master, the prophet Elisha?

**MESSENGER**

MESSENGER slams the door in NAAMAN's face.

Just a moment.

**NAAMAN**

NAAMAN is indignant.

Well, she at least could've asked me to come in.

**MESSENGER**

MESSENGER returns and opens the door.

My master says to tell you, "Go wash yourself seven times in the Jordan River, and you'll be healed."

SKIT SEVENTEEN: TAKE A BATH

MESSENGER shuts the door in
NAAMAN's face after speaking.

NAAMAN stands staring at the door and
then speaks.

## NAAMAN

Well! Of all the nerve! That prophet didn't
even come out and look at me! The least he
could've done is come out and wave his
arms around while he called on his God to
heal me. He's a quack! This is another lame-
brain idea!

NAAMAN turns and starts walking to exit
stage left.

**"Naaman, take a bath!" sign appears,
and the audience responds. Sign exits.**

NAAMAN looks at audience and then
continues walking to exit stage left.

Take a bath? Now that's a dumb idea!

**"Naaman, take a bath!" sign appears,
and the audience responds. Sign exits.**

NAAMAN turns as if talking to the audience.

Have you seen the water in the Jordan
River? If I wanted to take a bath, I could get
cleaner in the beautiful rivers at home.

**"Naaman, take a bath!" sign appears,
and the audience responds. Sign exits.**

NAAMAN goes off stage left, grumbling
all the way.

**(Grumbles)** Of all the bad ideas...

## SCENE 2: Back Home

 **Play track 22 on CD B.**

NAAMAN enters from stage right and
moves toward center stage.

## NAAMAN

It sure is good to be home.

SERVANT hurries in from stage right.

## SERVANT

Master, master, were you healed?

NAAMAN looks at the adhesive bandages on his body.

**NAAMAN**

Does it look like I was healed? That crackpot didn't even come out to see me. Of all the nerve! He just told me to go take a bath in the Jordan River!

SERVANT leans in toward NAAMAN to ask the question.

**SERVANT**

And did you?

NAAMAN turns his back on the SERVANT.

**NAAMAN**

Why would I want to do a silly thing like that?

**SERVANT**

Well, since you went to all that trouble to look him up, you might as well give it a try. After all, he's a man of God.

NAAMAN turns back to the SERVANT and taps his head while thinking.

**NAAMAN**

Let me think about it for a while.

*"Naaman, take a bath!" sign appears, and the audience responds. Sign exits.*

I guess this is no crazier than camel spit.

NAAMAN and SERVANT exit stage left.

**SCENE 3: The Jordan River**

 *Play track 23 on CD B. Puppeteers wave a blue sheet up and down.*

NAAMAN enters from stage left and looks down at the water. He bows his head to pray.

**NAAMAN**

Dear God, I never expected someone to tell me to take a bath in a river for a cure. Nothing else has worked, so I guess I'll give you a try. Amen.

*"Naaman, take a bath!" sign appears, and the audience responds. Sign exits.*

**121**

NAAMAN wades into the water up to his neck.

***Sign "One" appears, and the audience responds. Sign exits. NAAMAN disappears below the water and then comes up.***

Repeat for all seven signs.

Each time NAAMAN dips down below stage, a puppeteer removes one of NAAMAN's adhesive bandages until he comes up clean.

NAAMAN looks at his arms and body.

NAAMAN looks up toward heaven and then exits stage left praising God.

## NAAMAN
Well, it's all up to you now, God.

I'm healed! God, you work in the most unexpected ways. You are the one true God, and Elisha is your prophet. Hallelujah! Hallelujah!

**THE END!**

# Smelly Belly

**Topic:** God's Way

**Scriptures You Might Read:** Jonah 1–3; 2 Peter 3:9

**Scene:** In the belly of a big fish

**Characters**
**JONAH:** a reluctant prophet
**GOD'S VOICE:** heard off stage

**Props:** You'll need a Bible costume and four poster-board signs attached to sticks: One sign says, "We're here, Jonah!" the others are pictures of a bottle, a fish, and a beach ball (pp. 12-13).

**Setup:** Enlarge and attach the bottle, fish, and beach ball pictures to separate sticks. Dress Jonah in a Bible costume (such as a robe or a piece of fabric draped over his forehead and secured with yarn). Give the signs to two puppeteers, and have them sit backstage.

Before the skit, practice shouting with the audience, "We're here, Jonah!"

 **SCRIPT**

| ACTIONS | WORDS |
|---|---|
|  **Play track 24 on CD B.** | |
| ***Turn on a spotlight, or open the puppet stage curtains.*** | **JONAH** |
| | OK, Jonah, OK, here we go. It's time to open your eyes and get your first glimpse of heaven. That cold water and big fish thing were pretty scary, but it's gonna be all worth it when you see heaven. OK, here goes! |
| JONAH is standing with his head bowed or his hands covering his eyes. | |
| JONAH starts to uncover his eyes but changes his mind and covers them again. He shakes his head. | No, I can't look! I'm just too excited! Just think of all the years I've waited to get to see heaven, and now I'm finally here. It's going to be so wonderful! |
| JONAH jumps up and down in anticipation. | But I just have to look. Even though heaven will last forever and ever, I don't want to miss a single minute of it. All right now, on the count of three, I'll open my eyes. One...two...three! |

| | |
|---|---|
| JONAH uncovers his eyes and raises his hands in the air. | **JONAH**<br>Heaven! |
| JONAH looks around then hangs his head in disappointment. | Gee, heaven is really different than I thought it would be. |
| JONAH watches as **a bottle floats by, entering from stage right and exiting stage left.** | I didn't realize it would be so...so wet! |
| JONAH looks at his hands. | I'm already starting to get pruney! |
| JONAH looks around. **A beach ball floats by, entering from stage right and exiting stage left.** | I wonder where everybody else is? Probably out swimming or snorkeling somewhere. **(Yelling)** Hey! Is there anybody out there? |
| **"We're here, Jonah!" sign enters, and the audience responds. Sign exits.** | I thought I heard something, but with all of this dripping, I'm not sure. **(Yelling)** Hey! If you're there, don't whisper! Speak up! |
| **"We're here, Jonah!" sign enters, and the audience responds. Sign exits.** | No, I guess not. Wait a minute... |
| **A fish swims by, entering from stage right and exiting stage left.** | Oh, it was only you. I can't figure it. I sure didn't expect heaven to look like this. And I didn't think it would sound so sloshy. I certainly didn't think it would feel so slimy or smell so...so...so...ugh! |
| JONAH puts his hand to his head. | OK, Jonah, think, think. You were on that boat going to Tarshish. A big storm came up, and the sailors agreed when you said you were causing God to send the storm. Then they threw you overboard, and that big fish had you for supper. That was pretty interesting. But, hey, dying is part of the road to heaven. |
| JONAH looks around. | **(Sighs)** Yep, I'm surely dead, so this must be...But it doesn't look or sound or feel or smell like heaven. And I'm not gonna try it, but I'm betting it doesn't taste like heaven either! I don't get it! If this isn't heaven, then where could it be? |

| | |
|---|---|
| JONAH shows fear by trembling. | **JONAH**<br>Oh, no! Not there! I'm supposed to go to heaven when I die, not you know...the other place! **(Fearfully shouts)** *Oh, God! Where are you?* |
| JONAH jumps when he hears God's voice. | **GOD'S VOICE**<br>I'm here, Jonah. |
| | **JONAH**<br>**(Talking fast)** Oh, there you are. There's been some terrible kind of mistake. You see, I was supposed to go to heaven, but somehow my record got mixed up with someone else's. There's probably some really rotten guy from Nineveh walking around heaven right now. And I accidentally got sent down here, when I was supposed to go up to heaven. Isn't that funny, Lord? **(Laughs half-heartedly.)** |
| | **GOD'S VOICE**<br>Funny. Yes, funny. Funny you should mention Nineveh. I thought you were supposed to go there. |
| JONAH acts nervous, looks up and then down. | **JONAH**<br>Oh, yeah, about that. It was a funny thing about that. You see, I went to get my ticket to Nineveh, and when I got to the ticket window, the word Tarshish just popped out of my mouth. So I thought I'd just go to Nineveh by way of Tarshish. Isn't that funny, God? |
| | **GOD'S VOICE**<br>Funny? Funny how Tarshish is in the opposite direction from Nineveh. |
| JONAH holds his hands together. | **JONAH**<br>Good point. But, Lord, you didn't send me here for all of eternity for that, did you? |

**GOD'S VOICE**

No, I didn't. I sent you here to get your attention and to teach you a lesson.

**JONAH**

Well, you've certainly got my attention, Lord. So what's the lesson?

**GOD'S VOICE**

Tell me what you've learned, my son.

JONAH raises his hands and then lowers them.

**JONAH**

Let's see. I've learned that, when you tell me to do something, I should do it right away, even if I'm scared or didn't really want to. I've learned that your way is the best way. And I've learned that I don't ever, ever want to come back here again.

JONAH shakes his head for emphasis.

**GOD'S VOICE**

(**Laughs**) Where do you think you are?

**JONAH**

Where else?

JONAH opens his mouth in surprise.

**GOD'S VOICE**

You're in the belly of a great fish!

**JONAH**

The belly of a fish! No wonder this doesn't smell like heaven.

JONAH looks around in disgust.

**GOD'S VOICE**

Now *that's* funny! (**Laughs**)

**JONAH**

Wait, God! How do I get back to Nineveh?

**FISH**

Burp!

SKIT EIGHTEEN: SMELLY BELLY

JONAH, FISH, BEACH BALL and BOTTLE surge and exit off stage.

*Turn off the spotlight or shut the puppet stage curtains.*

**JONAH**
No way! Whooa!

**THE END!**

SKIT EIGHTEEN: SMELLY BELLY

# Hector

**Topic:** God's Love
**Scriptures You Might Read:** Jonah 3:10–4:11; 2 Peter 3:9

**Scene:** The school playground

**Characters**
**MARKY:** a girl who's wondering what friend to invite to church
**MADDIE:** another girl who's wondering the same thing

**Props:** You'll need the playground background (p. 8) and a poster-board sign on a stick that says, "Yes, Hector!"

**Setup:** Give the signs to a puppeteer, and have him or her sit backstage.

Before the skit, practice saying the words on the sign with the audience.

---

## SCRIPT

| ACTIONS | WORDS |
|---|---|
|  **Play track 25 on CD B.** | |
| MADDIE and MARKY enter from opposite sides of the puppet stage. MADDIE waves at MARKY. | |
| MARKY returns the wave, and they meet center stage. | **MARKY**<br>Hey, Maddie! Say, are you bringing a friend to church this Sunday? |
| MADDIE scratches her head as she wonders what MARKY is talking about. | **MADDIE**<br>Bring a friend to church? |
| MARKY nods her head "yes." | **MARKY**<br>Yeah! Remember? We're all supposed to invite someone to come to Sunday school with us this Sunday. |
| MADDIE shakes her head "no" and hangs her head a little. | **MADDIE**<br>Oh, yeah. Well, I don't think I'm going to ask anyone. |

| | |
|---|---|
| MARKY looks directly at her. | **MARKY**<br>Why not? |
| MADDIE shuffles back and forth. | **MADDIE**<br>Well...Well, what if the person makes fun of me for going to church? |
| | **MARKY**<br>How many times has that happened? And even if it does, so what? Isn't there anyone you can think of to invite to church? |
| MADDIE thinks a moment and then bobs up and down in excitement. | **MADDIE**<br>Um...uh...Oh! Oh! I know who I can ask. |
| | **MARKY**<br>Who? |
| MADDIE nods her head. | **MADDIE**<br>I'll ask Bethany. |
| | **MARKY**<br>Bethany Patterson? |
| MADDIE nods her head again. | **MADDIE**<br>Yeah, I know she'll come to church with me. |
| MARKY tilts her head to one side as she asks the question. | **MARKY**<br>But doesn't Bethany go to the Community Church in town? |
| MADDIE nods her head and points to herself. | **MADDIE**<br>Yeah! Her father is the pastor. She won't say "no," and she won't make fun of me. |
| MARKY shakes her head and sighs. | **MARKY**<br>I see. |
| MADDIE points to MARKY. | **MADDIE**<br>Who are you going to invite, Marky? |

| | **MARKY** |
|---|---|
| MARKY points to herself. | I'm inviting Hector! |
| MADDIE turns her head sharply to look at MARKY in surprise. | **MADDIE** Hector? Hector? Punching-Bag Hector? |
| MARKY nods her head. | **MARKY** Yes, Hector. |
| MADDIE shakes her head in disbelief. | **MADDIE** Oh, boy. I can't believe you're going to ask Punching-Bag Hector to come to church. |
| | **MARKY** Why not? |
| | **MADDIE** Well, for starters, Hector is the meanest, baddest bully in school. |
| MARKY shrugs. | **MARKY** So? |
| MADDIE steps closer to MARKY. | **MADDIE** So? So? Didn't Hector trip you in the hall at school? You fell down, spilling your lunch bag. |
| | **MARKY** Well, yes. |
| MADDIE steps even closer. | **MADDIE** Then, didn't he step on your peanut butter and banana sandwich and squish it all over the floor? |
| MARKY nods her head. | **MARKY** Yeah. |

| | |
|---|---|
| MADDIE steps even closer. | **MADDIE**<br>Then, Mr. Payton, the principal, came out of the office to see what was going on and he slipped on the squished sandwich and fell right on his nose. And didn't Hector blame *you* for it? |
| MADDIE leans so close that MARKY is almost doing a backbend. | |
| MARKY steps back and hangs her head while nodding. | **MARKY**<br>Well, yes, Hector did put the blame on me. |
| MADDIE points to MARKY. | **MADDIE**<br>You're making a big mistake asking Punching-Bag Hector to come to church with you. I wouldn't ask him if I were you. |
| *"Yes, Hector!" sign appears, and the audience responds. Sign exits.* | |
| | **MARKY**<br>Why not? |
| MADDIE shakes her head. | **MADDIE**<br>'Cause he'll probably make fun of you. He won't go to church. |
| MARKY looks up while thinking. | **MARKY**<br>Hmm...Well, who should I ask? |
| MADDIE taps her head while thinking. | **MADDIE**<br>Well, let's see...ah...You could ask Lori or Bobby or Latisha. |
| | **MARKY**<br>But they go to their own churches with their families. No, I think I'll stick with Hector. |
| *"Yes, Hector!" sign appears, and the audience responds. Sign exits.* | |

MADDIE shakes her head.

**MADDIE**

I just don't get it, Marky. Why would you want to invite Punching-Bag Hector to church?

**MARKY**

Well, I've been praying for Hector.

MADDIE does a double take.

**MADDIE**

Praying for Hector?

MARKY nods her head.

**MARKY**

Yes, I've been praying for Hector. I think that if Hector knew how much Jesus loves him, he wouldn't be so mean.

MADDIE pauses while thinking.

**MADDIE**

Oh...hmm...I hadn't thought about that. But do you think Jesus really loves Hector?

**"Yes, Hector!" sign appears, and the audience responds. Sign exits.**

MARKY nods her head.

**MARKY**

Yes, of course, Jesus does. Jesus loves us even before we know who he is.

MADDIE taps her head while thinking.

**MADDIE**

Hmmm...Maybe I'll ask Cory to come to church with me. I don't think she ever goes to church. I bet she doesn't even know that Jesus loves her either.

**MARKY**

So, Maddie, do you think I should ask Hector to come to church this Sunday?

MADDIE nods her head vigorously.

**MADDIE**

Yes!

*"Yes, Hector!" sign appears, and the audience responds. Sign exits.*

MADDIE and MARKY exit together in the same direction.

**THE END!**

# House Plans

**Topic:** Good plans

**Scripture You Might Read:** Jeremiah 29:4-14

**Scene:** The church or meeting room

**Characters**

LENNY: a boy who tries to give a lesson on God's plans
LESTER: a boy who tries to help by bringing Lenny all kinds of house plans

**Props:** You'll need a small houseplant.

**Setup:** Have a large sheet of paper with lines sketched on it so it looks like a blueprint. When Lester brings in a houseplant, have a puppeteer backstage hold the plant so it looks like Lester is carrying it. Have another puppeteer pause and restart the CD when mentioned in the script.

Before the skit, tell the audience that Lenny and Lester will be asking questions and for them to be ready to answer.

······················· **SCRIPT** ·······················

| ACTIONS | WORDS |
|---|---|
|  **Play track 26 on CD B.**<br><br>LENNY enters and speaks to the audience. | **LENNY**<br>Hi, everyone! My name is Lenny. I'm wondering something. Do any of your families have *plans* for later today? |
|  **Stop the CD** after the question and wait for children to respond. **Then play track 27 on CD B.** | Wow, that's great! My family has *plans* too. We're going to Grandma Gillywilly's house.<br><br>Grandma Gillywilly always fixes chicken and dumplings when we visit. I plan to eat three plates full. Yummy! Yep, that's my plan for today. But I want to talk to you about another kind of plan. |

| | |
|---|---|
| LESTER enters and bounces crazily across the stage to LENNY. | **LESTER**<br>Hey, Lenny! What's up? |
| LENNY looks at the audience and slaps his head with his hand. | **LENNY**<br>Oh, no! It's Lester! |
| Then LENNY turns to face LESTER. | Hi, Lester. I was just about to tell everyone about a special kind of plan. |
| LESTER continues to bounce up and down. | **LESTER**<br>Can I help? |
| | **LENNY**<br>Well, I hadn't planned on it. Remember the last time you tried to help? |
| LESTER tilts his head when he asks the question. | **LESTER**<br>You mean when I was helping you cook pancakes and I got one stuck on the ceiling? |
| | **LENNY**<br>Well, I was thinking more about the part when I had to call 9-1-1. |
| | **LESTER**<br>Oh, yeah, that! We didn't plan for that, did we? So can I help? |
| LENNY looks back and forth between the audience and LESTER. | **LENNY**<br>Hmm...I suppose. |
| LESTER points to LENNY. | **LESTER**<br>So we're talking about plans, are we? Have I got a plan for you! |
| | **LENNY**<br>Actually, Lester, I had a certain special plan in mind that I wanted to talk about. |

| | |
|---|---|
| LESTER runs quickly across stage to exit. | **LESTER**<br>And I know just the plan you have in mind! |
| LENNY watches LESTER leave and raises his hand as if to stop him. | **LENNY**<br>But...but...oh...**(Sighs)** |
| LESTER returns with the blueprint-like sheet. | **LESTER**<br>Here it is! |
| LENNY looks at the plans. | **LENNY**<br>What is that, Lester? |
| | **LESTER**<br>It's a plan for building a house. |
| | **LENNY**<br>That is a plan, but... |
| LESTER races offstage. | **LESTER**<br>Oh, if you don't like this plan, then wait! I'll be right back! |
| LENNY stares after LESTER with his mouth open. | |
| LESTER quickly returns with the blueprint. | |
| LENNY looks at the plan. | **LENNY**<br>Oh, my! Lester, what kind of plan is that? |
| LESTER looks at the plan. | **LESTER**<br>It's a plan to build uh...uh...an ice cube house! Is that right, everyone? What do you think this plan is for? |

 **Stop the CD** after the question and wait for children to respond. **Then play track 28 on CD B.**

SKIT TWENTY: HOUSE PLANS

**LENNY**

It's an igloo, Lester. You're holding a plan to build an igloo. It's a house made out of packed blocks of snow.

**LESTER**

Is that the cool plan you were going to talk about?

LENNY looks at the plan and shakes his head.

**LENNY**

Not exactly...

LESTER runs offstage.

**LESTER**

OK, I gotcha!

LENNY looks at the audience.

**LENNY**

(**Exasperated sigh**) I tried to warn you.

LESTER returns with the blueprint.

**LESTER**

Now this is a hot plan!

LENNY looks at the plan.

**LENNY**

A plan for what?

LESTER looks at the plan.

**LESTER**

You know one of those...uh...Luluhona Hiki Tiki huts.

**LENNY**

It looks like a grass hut to me.

LESTER nods his head.

**LESTER**

Yep, it takes a lot of planning to build one of these.

LENNY shakes his head.

**LENNY**

Yes, but it's not...

LESTER races offstage.

**LESTER**

OK, OK, I get the picture. You want something a little homier.

| | |
|---|---|
| LENNY shakes his head again. | **LENNY**<br>Oh, no! Here we go again! |
| LESTER enters with the blueprint. | **LESTER**<br>And it comes with a puppy plan too! |
| | **LENNY**<br>Lester, that's a doghouse. It's not the kind of plan that I mean. |
| LENNY faces the audience. | Hey, kids, what kind of plans has Lester been showing us? |
|  **Stop the CD** after the question and wait for children to respond. **Then play track 29 on CD B.** | That's right! They are different kinds of house plans! |
| LESTER nods his head excitedly. | **LESTER**<br>Yep, and I got 'em from planmaker.com on the Internet! |
| | **LENNY**<br>But, Lester, there is only one real Plan Maker. You misunderstood me. You thought I said house plans but... |
| LESTER runs offstage. | **LESTER**<br>I misunderstood house plans? Oh! Oh! I think I've got it now! |
| LENNY hangs his head in exasperation. | **LENNY**<br>Argh! |
| LESTER returns, carrying a houseplant. | **LESTER**<br>How's this? |
| LENNY raises his hands in frustration. | **LENNY**<br>Oh, Lester! Not a house *plant* and not house *plans*, I've been wanting to talk about *God's plan*! |

SKIT TWENTY: HOUSE PLANS

LESTER acts as if he's handing the house-plant down to a puppeteer backstage.

**LESTER**
Well, why didn't you just say so in the first place?

LENNY shakes his head and starts to walk away.

**LENNY**
I give up!

Then turns and walks back to LESTER.

Now, Lester, please just listen for once in your life! Do you understand?

LESTER stands perfectly still, looking at the audience. He doesn't answer.

Well, do you?

LESTER remains quiet. LENNY shakes LESTER.

Lester? Lester?!

LESTER comes to life and looks at LENNY.

**LESTER**
What? What? I was listening! Wasn't that the plan?

LENNY turns to face the audience.

**LENNY**
Ahh! As I was saying, everyone, God has a wonderful plan for you and me. In Jeremiah 29:11, God says, "For I know the plans I have for you...plans to prosper you and not to harm you, plans to give you hope and a future."

LESTER looks at the audience and asks them a question.

**LESTER**
Cool! God has a special plan for each of our lives. What kinds of plans do you think God has for you?

 **Stop the CD,** and wait for kids to respond. **Then play track 30 on CD B.** LESTER points to audience and then to himself.

No matter what, we can remember that God has good plans for you and me.

LESTER looks at LENNY.

Say, Lenny, do you have any plans for tomorrow night?

**LENNY**

As a matter of fact, I don't.

**LESTER**

How about planning to have dinner with me? We can talk more about God's plans for our lives.

LENNY puts an arm around LESTER.

**LENNY**

That sounds great! What are you planning on fixing for dinner?

**LESTER**

Well, what about pancakes?

The two start to exit as LENNY speaks.

**LENNY**

Great! I'll plan on bringing a fire extinguisher.

**THE END!**

## Scripture Index

## Topical Index

Group Publishing, Inc.
Attention: Product Development
P.O. Box 481
Loveland, CO 80539
Fax: (970) 679-4370

# Evaluation for
## *Just Add Puppets*

Please help Group Publishing, Inc. continue to provide innovative and useful resources for ministry. Please take a moment to fill out this evaluation and mail or fax it to us. Thanks!

● ● ●

1. As a whole, this book has been (circle one)

not very helpful                                                     very helpful

1        2        3        4        5        6        7        8        9        10

2. The best things about this book:

3. Ways this book could be improved:

4. Things I will change because of this book:

5. Other books I'd like to see Group publish in the future:

6. Would you be interested in field-testing future Group products and giving us your feedback? If so, please fill in the information below:

Name _____

Church Name _____

Denomination _____ Church Size _____

Church Address _____

City _____ State _____ ZIP _____

Church Phone _____

E-mail _____

# Exciting Resources for Your Children's Ministry

## Sunday School Specials Series

Lois Keffer

This best-selling series is a lifesaver for small churches that combine age groups...large churches that host family nights...and small groups with kids to entertain. Each book provides an entire quarter of active-learning experiences, interactive Bible stories, life applications, and take-home handouts. Children love them because they're fun and you'll love the easy preparation!

| | |
|---|---|
| Sunday School Specials | ISBN 1-55945-082-7 |
| Sunday School Specials 2 | ISBN 1-55945-177-7 |
| Sunday School Specials 3 | ISBN 1-55945-606-X |
| Sunday School Specials 4 | ISBN 0-7644-2050-X |

## The Children's Worker's Encyclopedia of Bible-Teaching Ideas

You get over 350 attention-grabbing, active-learning devotions...art and craft projects...creative prayers...service projects...field trips...music suggestions...quiet reflection activities...skits...and more—winning ideas from each and every book of the Bible! Simple, step-by-step directions and handy indexes make it easy to slide an idea into any meeting—on short notice—with little or no preparation!

| | |
|---|---|
| Old Testament | ISBN 1-55945-622-1 |
| New Testament | ISBN 1-55945-625-6 |

## 5-Minute Messages for Children

Donald Hinchey

It's easy to share meaningful messages that your children will enjoy and remember! Here are 52 short, Bible-based messages for you to use in Sunday school, children's church, or midweek meetings.

| | |
|---|---|
| | ISBN 1-55945-030-4 |
| 5-Minute Messages and More | ISBN 0-7644-2038-0 |

## Just-Add-Kids Games for Children's Ministry

If your classroom is stocked with the basics (chairs, paper, a light switch and masking tape) then you've got everything you need to play dozens of great new games! You get high-energy games...low-energy games...and everything in between. Some games have Bible applications, some require no supplies at all, and every game takes just moments to explain.

| | |
|---|---|
| | ISBN 0-7644-2112-3 |

Order today from your local Christian bookstore, or write: Group Publishing, P.O. Box 485, Loveland, CO 80539.

# More Resources for Your Children's Ministry

## Quick Children's Sermons 2: Why Did God Make Mosquitoes?

Now you're ready to answer some of the most common questions kids ask about God...Jesus...heaven...and life as they observe it. You get 50 befuddling questions straight from the lips of God's smallest saints...and great answers, too! Use this warm, witty book as a year's supply of children's sermons...for Sunday school...or to launch discussions in class or children's church!

ISBN 0-7644-2052-6

## Crazy Clothesline Characters

Carol Mader

You're already familiar with these Bible stories—The Creation, Noah's Ark, Nebuchadnezzar, Jonah, Jesus' Birth, The Prodigal Son, and 34 others. But now you have 40 new and fun ways to tell them to your children! You'll tell stories with cue cards, food, walks, flashlights, balloons, and other multi-sensory items to involve children in the story...and to help them remember it for a lifetime!

ISBN 0-7644-2140-9

## The Ultimate Bible Guide for Children's Ministry

You want your kids to know the difference between the Old and New Testaments. To quickly and easily find Bible verses. To understand the Bible and be comfortable exploring God's Word. Start here! These kid-friendly 5- to 15-minute activities help children from preschool through 6th grade master the skills that make Bible reading fun. Give kids a rock-solid foundation for using the Bible—and do it without boring kids.

ISBN 0-7644-2076-3

## Amazing Science Devotions for Children's Ministry

Kids love figuring out how stuff works, so put their natural curiosity to work! From "What makes popcorn pop?" to "Where do rainbows come from?," here's tons of science fun that connects kids with God's wonderful world. For children's sermons...Sunday school...midweek programs and clubs...anywhere you want to give kids' faith a boost and help them learn about God!

ISBN 0-7644-2105-0

Discover our full line of children's, youth, and adult ministry resources at your local Christian bookstore, or write: Group Publishing, P.O. Box 485, Loveland, CO 80539. www.grouppublishing.com